I don't know
where I'm going
but I want to be

there

A TRAMPOLINE FOR THE MIND

This is a book that wants to be a visually associative, leaf-through timeline. The written contributions explore ideas such as data manipulation, collaborative design, mental ecology, and generational design-notions, which the authors consider to be stepping stones for tomorrow's visual practitioners.

This book doesn't pretend to be complete, nor does it claim that the associations in meaning, which it hopefully triggers in its reader, are the only possible ones. On the contrary: the visual matches in this book reflect nothing more than the subjective perspectives of the editors.

This book wants to be a trampoline for like minds. The choice, selection, and coupling of images came about by asking ourselves what the essence of each image is, and then trying to find a historical (backwards) or contemporary (forward) equivalent of that characteristic.

Sometimes a visual similarity hides a divergence in intention, approach, or impact. Sometimes images converge content-wise but look very different at first sight. It's the magic of visual rhetoric, and probably one of the most challenging aspects of graphic design: to produce meaning, instantaneously, between medium and audience.

"Somewhere along the line I knew

ere'd be girls, visions, everything;

somewhere along the line the pea

ould be handed to me." JACK KEROUAC, ON THE ROAD (1957)

GRAPHIC DESIGN MUSEUM

The Graphic Design Museum, the only museum in the world for graphic design, is a platform for graphic design, the professional field for visual communication. It offers an international podium for established designers and is, in addition, a platform for new top talent. In the museum, new forms of visual communication such as Internet are linked to the history of graphic design.

Graphic design has been around for about 100 years and has built up a rich tradition in the Netherlands with internationally renowned designers. In the twentieth century, graphic design was a fairly prescribed area with a small group of professional practitioners such as Piet Zwart, Willem Sandberg, Wim Crouwel, and Anthon Beeke. This history is the foundation of the museum and acts as reference for new developments in the dynamic graphic image culture.

Temporary exhibitions in the Graphic Design Museum always clearly make a link with the history of graphic design. In this way, we do complete justice to our theme: 'Connecting the past and the future'. We show how new fields of graphic design, such as data visualisation, arise and develop. With our temporary exhibitions, we try to impart a certain recognition to our visitors, which allows them to delve deeper so that they can be amazed at the dynamic profession that is graphic design.

The museum carefully builds up an important collection in order to develop further in our international ambition and position in the coming years. The museum's collection contains on the one hand historical and contemporary physical objects (such as printed material and posters) and on the other a database with digital material such as illustrations of websites, film, animation, and images that have never appeared in a physical form.

The museum regularly exhibits the material.

Visitors to the Graphic Design Museum become aware of the power of images. They experience that images can do something with them and also that they can do something with images.

This shows the strength of this profession.

Initiator: Graphic Design Museum / Mieke Gerritzen
Concept: Sophie Krier, Marjolijn Ruyg
Editors: Minke Kampman, Marjolijn Ruyg, Sophie Krier
Design: Marjolijn Ruyg
Texts: Bas van Lier, Lotte van Gelder, Luna van Loon
Essays: Edial Dekker, Julian Bittiner, Mieke Gerritzen, Thomas Lommee, Victor Margolin, Willem Schinkel, David Stairs, Annelys de Vet, Micah White
Translator: Jonathan Ellis

Thanks to: Hanna Aerts, Fabienne van Beek, Anna Thalia Benus, Gina van Beuningen, Ronald Boer, Fran van den Bogaert, Max Bruinsma, Liz Davis, Kees Dorst, Amanda Elshout, Luc Goderie, Hendrik-Jan Grievink, Henk Groenendijk, Erik Kessels, Koert van Mensvoort, Kali NIkitas, Novak Ontwerp, Niels Schrader, Martijn van der Sluis, David Smeulders, Studio Beige, Robbert van Strien, John Thackara, Roland Warners, Koehorst in t' Veld, Coralie Vogelaar, Willem van Weelden, Thomas Widdershoven

Printed by Ofset Yapimevi, Turkey

Publisher: BIS Publishers, Amsterdam
Building Het Sieraad
Postjesweg 1, 1057 DT Amsterdam
The Netherlands
T (31) 020 515 02 30, F (31) 020 515 02 39
bis@bispublishers.nl, www.bispublishers.nl

ISBN 978-90-6369-257-5

"What's your road, man? - Holyboy road, madman road, rainbow road, guppy road, any road. It's an anywhere road for anybody anyhow."

JACK KEROUAC, ON THE ROAD (1957)

GRAPHIC DESIGN WONDERLAND

CONNECTING THE PAST AND THE FUTURE

Mieke Gerritzen

The world of graphic design, the profession for visual communication, part of a worldwide network, is a sanctuary for text and image, for dynamism and change. With a proliferation of styles, ideas, opinions, and methods, graphic design is part of the bombardment of images taking place all around us. Media is becoming increasingly visual and our environment is becoming media.

We are adrift in an image culture, with buildings, information, cars, fashion, products, and art all communicating with us. The explosive growth of artistic production in the last 10 years has had an enormous influence on the traditional art and design world. The new generation of professional artists and designers has grown up with internet, mobile telephones, and virtual worlds. Today's professionals create their own context and do not, by definition, aspire to connect with the established cultural elite such as museums. A new world has arisen around the idea of Graphic Design because the profession has immediately undergone the effects of the digital revolution. It influences the aestheticising of society, the creative industry, and the way people connect and communicate with each other via the (social) media. The profession continues to develop and reacts to technological developments and everybody participates. There is no new definition for the dynamic Graphic Design. It moves.

That which until the nineties appeared to be a small craftsman-like and cultural profession, seems, in the 21st century, to have grown into a democratised discipline with a central position in modern media. *'I don't know where I'm going but I want to be there'* is the reaction to this development. It tells something about the history of graphic visual culture and lets us see where we are now. The tradition of printed material has made way for visual communications in a dynamic media world.

It emerged as a very young discipline at the beginning of the 20th century, in the period when art movements such as DADA, De Stijl and Bauhaus took

shape. Important developments for the freedom of the design. Beauty, social awareness, resistance, criticism but also commerce, theory, art, and a cross-discipline mentality came together in this period. Only after the second world war did the profession acquire a depth and rules and contexts were set.
A professional association was formed, graphic design became a recognised course at art academies and ambitious designers developed various visions about the profession. They kept graphic design alive and active and initiated a broad social discussion during the 'seventies and 'eighties.

The arrival of the Internet at the start of the 'nineties brought a tremendous change: everybody communicated now using images. There are countless people active with it throughout the world; for example, the British student Alex Tew designed a website many years ago where companies could advertise and this made him both famous and a millionaire.

The professional designer is again searching for the meta position. But this new generation of designers is not so much looking for a way to develop their own visual language, but regard the design process rather as juggling and remixing existing material. They combine and manipulate existing styles and are often totally unaware of the fact that the images with which they work were also once developed by designers. But through lack of knowledge they often cannot make the reference to their predecessors.

The older generation of designers cannot really place the rich current remixed image. These renowned designers from the past have, with their designs, built up their own style or visual language to which they can claim authorship and to which they owe their fame They are often famous image icons such as posters with political messages and successful logo designs. 'I Don't Know Where I'm Going But I Want To Be There' makes, with this publication, a connection between the original work made in the 20th century and the new work of the 21st century. These image matches offer current work a context and bring work from the past up to date.

Welcome in Graphic Design Wonderland: a broad area where designers at their own initiative or as the result of a commission take the freedom to develop personal fascinations. They present minor and major social discussion points and are capable of translating changes and opinions in our society into a powerful and exceptional image. Sometimes in the form of a product, sometimes by making extremely complex information accessible and sometimes simply by looking or experiencing.
Designers create a new market of cultural production with their own ideas, their feeling for engagement, with a characteristic visual language and with their own opinions about how media influences and directs our lives.

It is graphic designers who, from the centre of media and the arts, look at the world of culture and see just how large it has become.

"We were all delighted, we all realized we were leaving confusion and nonsense behind and performing our one noble function of the time, move."

JACK KEROUAC, ON THE ROAD (1957)

THE BIG AND THE SMALL D

IF I CAN REPAIR THE MACHINE,
I CAN MAKE THE MACHINE

Sophie Krier

Transcript of a conversation with Victor Margolin, Chicago, July 26, 2010.

Caribou Coffee, 8th ST. and Wabash Ave. Victor Margolin, design historian, emeritus professor at the University Of Illinois, Chicago, fervent collector of ethnic kitsch ('I collect souvenirs and photos of restaurant facades, in search of the codes that mark a place or a restaurant as Chinese or Mexican. You want to mark something as being Mexican, and you get this certain typeface with all these things bursting from it; the codes are mostly very cliché') and author of a three-volume book that will be published in several years, the World History of Design, *orders an espresso at the counter – Diane serves it to him in a ceramic cup, a rare sight in the United States. 'This is one of the only places where they'll still make me one like this.'*

SK: There are a couple a questions I'd like us to start off with, such as "Why another museum?", "Why a museum of Graphic Design in the 20th Century?", and, if we manage to answer that, then I want to talk about the 'how' part… How should such a museum be envisioned, not only as a place but also as a space of activity and as a collection? And what does this say about design practices of tomorrow?

VM: My personal canon would be the best that was done in different situations and contexts, whether the Western, Middle Eastern, or African context. And I'd say there are multiple tasks at hand for a museum today. First, to be a place where you can see worthy original works. There's no debate about this, and museums are good at showing such work. Second, the museum should be a place to see work you might not see anywhere else. In the Netherlands, it would be great to see an exhibition of Arabic type or Nigerian barbershop signs. Third, by virtue of curatorial strategy, museums need to argue for new ways to look at and think about graphic design, which means novel ways of exhibiting work, and of showing pieces in relation to one another. A museum can create a narrative out of a body of objects. Often these are boring narratives, locked into the grand old stories. Mixing the high and the low and the popular, as commentaries and counter-commentaries, would open things up.

SK: I'd also like to talk about the importance of history and graphic design history in particular, in terms of learning it, and relating to it from your own practice. What can graphic design as a profession learn from its own history? Where is graphic design standing now and what do you see as tasks at hand for the profession in the future? But first in relation to your project: why another history, and why did you scrap the word 'graphic' and add the word 'world' in your title?

VM: Well the two aren't antithetical. My book, the World History Of Design, really deals with graphic design and product design. You could throw in architecture and engineering and other things as well but there are already detailed histories of those subjects. To me it doesn't make sense to isolate one medium from another, because you have so many practitioners who historically have worked across various media. So to think of Henri van de Velde as a graphic designer doesn't really make a lot of sense. That was a minor part of his oeuvre. You have to see him in the context of Art Nouveau. I don't think you should study his lettering in terms of its effect on the reader but instead see it as an extension of the aesthetic values which he invested in his Bloemenwerf House - his wife's clothing, his furniture, etc. And I think the notion of a visual wholeness is very much a turn of the century phenomenon. So to me it doesn't make sense to slice off one part of a designer's work for a field called graphic design or product design and simply leave the rest in the dust.

As historians we work like curators, because we pick things, we make chronologies out of them and then we have to make histories out of them by giving the chronologies a meaning. You always have to be able to justify what you put in your narrative. So for instance, if you take Cassandre or Piet Zwart, you try to discover the thought process they used in putting their pieces together. Piet Zwart had very strong ideas about being modern. Modern in that time generally was reflected, maybe in a reductive way, in sans serif as opposed to serif typefaces. Zwart was interested in a typeface that had no reference to the past. He also thought that rhetoric as an argument could be more plastic. So he said (and he took a lot of his cues from Lizzitsky who was more of a theorist while Piet Zwart was a refined craftsman), why do we have to experience words in a linear sequence? Why do words all have to be the same size? And what you get is a shift from the idea that typography is verbal to the idea that it is visual. And once you shift to the visual you start asking questions about the limitations of the verbal. Piet Zwart liked the fact that you could take all these minimal elements and get other things out of them. So he did over six hundred ads for The Dutch Cable Company that carried nearly the same message. Each one was a variant of the others. Zwart was basically asking himself: how many ways can I get these simple elements to work within a single set of parameters. I use historical examples in this way to demonstrate how thought processes and modes of investigation work.

In terms of understanding design, I believe designers need to locate themselves in an historical narrative. In design education in Latin America, for example, students are learning the design history of Europe and America, and even though their countries are becoming more important in a global sense, Latin American design history is still excluded from the dominant design history narratives. That's the old colonial model: the only thing that counts is the centre. Last May I gave a keynote address at a conference of Turkish design historians in Izmir. The title of my paper was The Other Design History. My point was that the story has to be enlarged, the narratives have to be multiplied, and that we need the bigger picture to see how the back and forth works between the different cultures that participated in it.

SK: In your conference paper entitled Building a Design Research Community[1], you mention the importance of "engaging with the full scope of things", and you also state that design research should prioritise issues over methods.

VM: Yes. I really don't support the idea of separate graphic design histories or industrial design histories. Graphic design history is a whole industry and has a very strong culture. Its exponents tend to get very clubby about it. I am interested in a broader view of design. As a concept, you could get me to talk about very obscure things like fire hydrants or bicycle racks; I look at all of those things. I find great satisfaction in looking across the whole spectrum of design. So if you talk about Gerrit Rietveld's Red and Blue Chair for instance, you're concerned with the same issues as when you're talking about Piet Zwart ads – the same things are at work and I think the difference of dimensions isn't such a big deal. So to return to your question, I think we need a design history that can prepare students and practitioners to feel comfortable moving from one field to another. This is much more valuable than a history that simply isolates one group of artefacts.

SK: Could you say something about how you go about this inclusiveness in your own world history? Is it a rumour that you go back thirty thousand years ago? I mean how many world views can you include in such a project?

VM: The structure of the book is like this, like a V.

SK: It starts small and it grows big.

VM: Yes. I don't spend a lot of time talking about cave paintings or flint stones and all that. However, it's important to start at the beginning and to show that there is something called evolution, of course. So I talk briefly about things that are already well-known, like the shifts from pictograms to cuneiform writing. What I really want to talk about is how we get to

Latin letters, and how we get to other alphabets. So I write about Arabic, Hebrew, Japanese, and Chinese. I found it to be possible, using the work of other scholars, to show how these alphabets have changed over time and when they were first cast as metal types for printing.

What you see, for example, early in the 20th Century in Shanghai, which was the commercial centre of China at that time, is that when modernisation arrives – you'll find it happening in different places at different times, in different ways – there is an interest in modernising traditional Chinese type that is based on calligraphy. So typographers then start looking at Western modern types, and adapting elements from those to Chinese characters. Then you get strange hybrids. Or in Indian advertising posters of the 1930s you have lettering artists taking elements from Art Deco alphabets and adapting them to Hindi scripts. Similarly, in the 1920s you see that the Japanese Avant Garde is very interested in Russian constructivism so you have Japanese artists copying Rodchenko's bold Cyrillic lettering style in Japanese characters. So once you start moving around cultures like that, you find all these strange hybrids that I think are fascinating.

So why a world history? Because, at least in my argument, design with a small d is happening everywhere all the time. The small d is basically what people do to survive. You'll find in Africa in the 18th and 19th Century complete systems of artefact production and dissemination, and then what happens during the colonialist period, is that Western goods start to drive out traditional craftsmen, and they come into conflict with design with a big d, which is mass production and so forth. Some believe that if we're going to write about design we should write about design only with a big D, so they start with the 18th Century in England, Wedgewood and then the 1851 exhibition… But while these things were happening there was design with a small d going on all over the world. According to the dominant definition of design, if you look at the African continent in the 18th Century, there is nothing happening. And this is a big problem.

SK: So your inclusive definition of design would be…

VM: The big and the small d. At any given time and any given place there is something called design. And that's what I'm looking for in the narrative of my book. So for example writing about China: the way industrial design begins to develop is that you begin with imported machines. This is standard in a lot of pre-industrial countries. Somebody brings in machines to set up a factory. Then local people learn to repair the machines. Then some entrepreneur says if I can repair the machine, I can make the machine. So he sets up a local factory to make the machines, and I call that a kind of design. First copying, then adding something new. The difficulty then lies in the infrastructure and the capital to get these things produced. But the point is that everywhere people are smart and they see things around them and they try to adapt. So part of what I deal with in the book is the economic and social structures in which design takes place. Because we in the West, being the heirs to the Enlightenment and the Industrial Revolution, grew up thinking that design is something natural. We don't even think that we can only do design the way we do it because we live in a set of economic and political and social conditions that made it possible and that are not replicated everywhere around the world. So we tend to naturalise these conditions, we tend to say, this is design, without realising that the Industrial Revolution came about through a specific set of conditions; and only the countries that could replicate them, like Germany, France, and the United States, were able to participate. Other people continued working in other sets of conditions. So it's important to understand that design is not a natural process. It's very much dependent on an economic system that involves banks, distribution channels etc. And it involves a democratic culture, where people are free to innovate. Of course, there is design in command economies too, but it's a different type of design.

So in the book, design is framed by nations for the most part until we get to globalisation. Because nations until recently are the ones that for the biggest part control the conditions within their borders through taxes, roads, and so on. So the book is about national policies and the ways in which design occurs within them. Therefore if I talk about Scandinavia in the 1920s and 1930s it's not just about style, it's about values that arise. So you have a tradition first of all of a relation to the environment, that is very different from the English one for instance. That relation tends to develop into a way of thinking about design as something that is real, not artificial, so you get the emphasis on wood and natural materials, and you get small scale democracies, in which it becomes possible to say "we can deliver a middle class life to almost everybody". So Scandinavians developed first the idea of natural materials and second the idea of good design for all. And that became a very distinct regional and cultural ideology that was not held by everybody else in the world. The French didn't believe it, and the Americans had other notions of democracy that were much more based on commercial interest.

So the book is framed by these conditions. At the same time I believe in the designer as an author, and I disagree with people who don't want to talk about production and look only at the consumer side. You need shared ideas about what to make for design to happen.

SK: There has to be intention, you mean?

VM: Yes, but I'm not a determinist. Nobody really knows how the constraints of these conditions work. And one thing designers do is push those constraints.

SK: So then it's a question of personal intent, character, will power, and ambition, to be able to push those limits and to be able to relate to them in an intelligent way.

VM: For a world history of anything it's important to frame national histories within a larger context, and to be aware that your experience at any given moment is matched by somebody else's experiences somewhere else, and it might be very different from yours, which means that there is a possibility that at some point they might intersect. So the more we know about other people's experience the more capable we are going to be in terms of how we function. Not only resourceful, but the more understanding and accommodating we are going to be. More and more people transcend national boundaries, their ethos and sensibilities are global, and this opens up new possibilities for design. Some of the most productive moments in history are when cultures have come into relation with each other, learnt something, and actually transformed each other. Differences have a value.

SK: Last year at the symposium *Me You And Everyone We Know Is A Curator*[2], Bruce Sterling was talking about the next big thing being a lot of small things. According to him, one of the most important directions we need to move into is to learn to make many more mistakes, a multitude of small mistakes, so that we can learn faster and move on more efficiently.

VM: I believe in individual initiative too, networks and community gardening and all that, but I think that we are at a point where it's very important to learn how to undertake large projects collectively, because some of the major things that need to be done require power at a different level than grass roots.

SK: I have a quote to support that argument, from Geoff Mulgan (which he said at the conference for Creative Innovation, 22 November 2007): "Social innovation depends on alliances between what could be called the 'bees' and the 'trees'. The bees are small organisations, individuals and groups, who have the new ideas, and are mobile, quick, and able to cross-pollinate. The trees are the big organisations – governments, companies, or big NGOs – which are poor(er) at creativity, but generally good at implementation, and have the resilience, roots, and scale to make things happen. Both need each other."

VM: There has never been a better moment for design; because on the one hand it's becoming much more diffuse. Designers have many resources to actualise and spread what they think is of value at a micro level. So on a small scale things have never been better. But when you move up the ladder, let's say to who decided to introduce all electric cars, it gets harder. This is a system level. I just read an article about the director of I-GO, a Car Sharing Enterprise, who decided to introduce all electric cars. This is a way to help a new market to grow. Designers have to learn to think more and more in terms of systems and large strategies. In terms of global design practices, you still need a personal narrative to wind your way through all the new possibilities at hand. There's always going to be a dialectic between the things that could be done and the things that it makes sense for you to do, without sticking on the narrow path, on the way you've got to take this from here and there and this means much more strategising and reflection and manoeuvring.

One of the things I ask when I conduct critiques with graphic design students, for example, is to "give me a justification for this typeface". It's not enough to say it's cool. You've got to get to that level of metaphor or meaning. Which means that you don't even want to look at a thousand typefaces, you'd rather look at thirty, because at the degree to which you have to interrogate them, it's simply not efficient to do that for a thousand typefaces! It's only efficient to deal with a certain scale. Emil Ruder said the Univers was the answer to everything, as long as there are thirty different point sizes we have the answer to everything. I don't believe in that at all. Typography can be very witty. You can set up a set of expectations and then subvert them. There are all sorts of rhetorical ways to use type. And if you think about it as rhetoric and the fact that the typeface has to argue for something, this has to motivate every thoughtful student to not look at everything and to cut out huge categories of typefaces, I mean, how else can you be a designer?

To get back to where we started, and I'll finish here, people always ask where design is going, as if design is something that has its own trail. It's not going anywhere. The question is where are we going, and where do we want to go, which I would argue is towards a more just, equitable, ecologically sound world.

SK: That ties in to something Micah White writes about in his contribution to this book, the notion of mental ecology, which should be nurtured as a counter reaction to the mental pollution engendered by today's information overload.

VM: Well I would argue with him that mental space is important. Because something new arises only when there is space for it.

1. First published as "Building a Design Research Community," in Design Plus Research: Proceedings of the Politecnico di Milano Conference, May 18-20, 2000, edited by Silvia Pizzocaro, Amilton Arruda and Dijon De Moraes (Milan: Politecnico di Milano, 2000).
2. Me You And Everyone We Know Is A Curator is a symposium about quality in the age of visual overload, which was organised by the Graphic Design Museum on 19 December, 2009 in Paradiso, Amsterdam.

"What is that feeling when you're driving away from people and they recede on the plain till you see their specks dispersing? – it's the too huge world vaulting us, and it's good-bye. But we lean forward to the next crazy venture beneath the skies."

JACK KEROUAC, ON THE ROAD (1957)

GENERATION: A MANIFESTO FOR LATENCY

FOR A CRITIQUE OF 'GENERATION'

Willem Schinkel

Let's start with a rupture. With a departure. A departure from the commonsensical Concept of 'generation'. Of 'a generation'. Used in its commonsensical way, 'generation' is either the name for a specific age cohort in general, or, more specifically, for a culturally defined age group. Let's leave that idea behind for the moment and think of 'generation' in the active sense.

'A generation' may be defined by its generation – that is, by what it generates – but one can only tell if 'a generation' actually existed until after the fact of generation. A generation in the sense of an age-cohort is thus quite a different thing from 'a generation' that has creatively generated. To speak of 'a generation' before it has generated is a way of classifying it, of cutting short its creative potential. It is possible, depending on what one generates, to form a 'generation of the mind' rather than of the 'body', of mere age. A generation of the mind comprises a unity of generation in the active sense, not in the temporal sense. One can be of the surrealist generation if one generates in a non-objectifying, dream-like way. There is a cross-temporal language of forms that can be generated, much like in Focillon's theory of form, forms are generated through historical time, each time actualised in new styles, because 'life is form, and form is the modality of life'[1]. To be 'of a certain generation' can thus be regarded in more substantial terms than is usually the case.

The commonsensical concept of 'a generation' certainly has its uses. It offers a classification, a reduction of complexity in that it provides a shorthand way of cataloguing oneself or others. It temporally fixes and thereby legitimates the origins of 'schools' – such as, in Dutch design, those of Van Toorn and Crouwel. It provides such schools with historical roots and this gives them plausibility as a 'school'. From a sociological perspective, the concept of generation is of the same class as 'school' or 'canon'. For such concepts to be productive, a certain rigidity, a quality of fixing, is necessary. And such fixing practices are everywhere in art, architecture, and, I presume, in design.

Any field of activity that autonomises and becomes a separate 'discipline', with its own professional training, its own canon, history, and hierarchy, is in desperate need of fixing concepts such as the commonsensical meaning of 'a generation'.

Generalised generation: design for latency

But a more substantial conception of 'generation' yields another view. Because in a sense, the idea of a 'generation in design' is tautological. Design is generation actively conceived. Let me venture an operational definition of design here. Let's consider design as a way of aesthetic generation according to recognised (and at least to some extent: recognisable) models. As such it is a way of imprinting memory in objects. The memory of a thing consists of its generation, which does not necessarily end with the design-cycle of conception-analysis-development-production, but which continues in its practical use. Memory, however, means forgetting. To remember is possible by forgetting the many things one doesn't need to remember. Remembering/forgetting is thus a way of selecting, of selectively accessing and of selectively directing attention. Our age is of special interest here because it is both an age of access and of attention. In such an age, everybody continually selects and generates. As Nietzsche predicted: the death of God means that man occupies his vacant place. Dasein has become design[2]. Today, in an age in which the Great Designer operating on the basis of the principle of 'Intelligent Design', no longer has credibility, everybody designs, and generation has become a generalised necessity. Generation is generalised, daily life consists of selecting, of forging meaning and use out of excessive access.

It is amidst these generalised powers of generation that design has emerged as a distinct discipline. One way of interpreting its rise is as a ratification and legitimisation of a generalised model of generation. At the same time, it draws lines through the generating mass, establishes ritualised procedures of generating, and it orders generation and attention through fashion and aesthetic hierarchisation. But in an age of excessive attention, when everything is manifest, there is no more need of manifestos. While architecture asserted itself as a discipline of manifestos, why would design bother? What we are rather in need of is latency. Latency is a principle of disrupting generation. A principle of indeterminacy, of not selecting, a principle of discontinuity that breaks the daily flow of generation rather than damming it according to models or fashions.

Why latency? Because generation has become generalised, fetishised. Generalised generation is more than the necessity of Dasein's Entwurf, it is more than Beuys' 'everyone is an artist' or than Arendt's homo faber. It is peculiarly connected to contemporary capitalism, which exploits individual creativity, spontaneity, generation. Capitalist generation, at least under conditions of 'cognitive capitalism'[3], is first and foremost the exploitation of a radically decentralised and individualised generation. Whereas the Fordist regime of accumulation generated collective identities, the Post-Fordist regime incites the self-generation of identities, paradoxically on massive scale. For the first time, 'mass production' actually means that the mass produces itself. Every-day life is a life of generation, but to a large extent of exploitable generation out of necessity.

Capitalism, exploitation… concepts that spoil parties. But whatever their cash-value, I would argue that an age of generalised generation is in need of latency. We need creative openings in continuous flows of generation. Per-haps, today, true access to creative forms of attention lies in the gaps, the spaces in-between that generalised generation continually threatens to fore-close. I propose to add to future discussion the idea that design must now first and foremost mean: the generation of the gap, the interval, the interruption of generation. It must embody its own undoing.

1. Focillon, H. (1989) The Life of Forms in Art, New York: Zone Books. —— (forthcoming) The Shape of Time: Remarks on the History of Things, New Haven: Yale University Press.
2. Oosterling, H. (2000) Radicale middelmatigheid, Amsterdam: Boom.
3. Fumagalli, A. & S. Mezzadra (2010) Crisis in the Global Economy: Financial Markets, Social Struggles, and New Political Scenarios, Los Angeles: Semiotext(e).

"Every now and then a clear harmonic cry gave new suggestions of a tune that would someday be the only tune in the world and would raise men's souls to joy."

JACK KEROUAC, ON THE ROAD (1957)

ECOLOGY OF IMAGE ECOLOGY OF MIND

ON THE FUTURE OF ACTIVISM

Micah White

Since the 1970s, a steady stream of environmentalist classics have foretold the day when rampant consumerism would bring humanity to the tipping point, and the precipice of collapse, in a world polluted beyond recovery. And after four decades of dire warnings, even the industrial capitalists who are to blame now assure us they agree. And yet, nothing has changed; onward the sinking ship drifts.

Our inability to avert catastrophe is due to the overly materialistic, scientific approach that environmentalism has taken. Concerning itself exclusively with contamination of our physical world while ignoring pollution of our mental world, environmentalism has addressed only one side of the problem. Frantically trying to ameliorate the symptoms of our ideologically bankrupt civilization-in-decline, we've left the temples of our minds unguarded, our imaginations open to pillage by any corporation with an advertising budget.

The world is awash in commercial imagery. Advertising is so prevalent that, to some, it is no longer visible. The result is a plague of consumerist fantasies that homogenise our dreams, commercialise our desires and pollute our mental ecology. We close our eyes, we see an ad. We hum a song, it's a jingle. Steadily, the unrelenting graphic assault trammels the wilderness of our souls. And as society descends toward financial, ecological, and moral collapse, we are paralysed by the visual pollution and commercial interjections that saturate our minds and chain us to the consumer trough.
Deploying thousands of commercial messages against our psyches each day, the advertising industry is running the most cynical psychological experiment ever imagined. We are a people propagandised from birth with slick pixel-perfect ads that sell simultaneously foot fungal cream and the American dream™. It is time to acknowledge the tragic psychic toll this is taking. Digitally manipulated imagery that defiles our mindscape with consumer-hype, fascist-cool and agro-sexuality is as toxic to our world as industrial chemicals are to our rivers.

Shifting the terrain of struggle to the mind calls for a rethinking of contemporary political and artistic engagement. That paradigm shift is now underway: a new generation of activists, designers, and visionaries are breaking through the false barrier that separates subjective and objective reality, personal and societal insanity, the distortion of mindscapes through advertising and destruction of landscapes through climate change. And in doing so, they are ushering in the future of activism as mental ecology, an environmentalism concerned with pollution of the mind.

Mental environmentalism challenges us to consider the consequences for civilisation of the consumerist fantasies that plague our minds. It proposes that when the minds of our neighbours are polluted, when their children know corporate logos but not the breeze of wild spaces, a psychic decimation of the world is accomplished, a desecration that manifests as increased consumption and its by-product, environmental degradation.

The activist of tomorrow will fight the pollution of our mental ecology before it results in catastrophes in our physical reality. But this struggle cannot be confined to the semiotic level; we'll need a spiritual insurgency against the polluters of our minds – corporations, advertisers, and consumerists alike. Speaking practically, a disruption, a jamming, a black-spotting will be necessary.

To disrupt this waking dream, it is not enough to say that we must design a different picture, change the order of the signs, or dream another world. Those words won't take us far if we do not stem the flow of images that saturate us, the marketing messages that commercialise us, the faux-news that distract us. These info-toxins are driving us insane and more: leaping from our psyches, they debase the world as well. No, we must do more than paint another layer on the canvas: we need to break the gilded frame.

"They have worries,
they're counting the miles,
they're thinking about where
to sleep tonight, how much
money for gas, the weather,
how they'll get there –
and all the time they'll get
there anyway, you see."

JACK KEROUAC, ON THE ROAD (1957)

DOES MONEY MANIPULATE DESIGN?

A DESIGNER'S TAKE ON THE ART WORKERS'S COALITION

Julian Bittiner

First published in Issue 14 of Graphic Mag as a studio 'motto', the above text is an adaptation of the original document Does Money Manipulate Art? from 1969. Bittiner discovered it thanks to the P.S.1. exhibition '1969'. Written by the Art Worker's Coalition, the original text addressed the increasingly irreconcilable views between artists and museums on the purpose and accessibility of art. Wondering to what extent these same questions might be directed towards designers, Julian Bittiner adapted the original text, replacing each instance of the word artist with the word designer, and making other amendements where needed for the sake of coherence.

Does money manipulate *clients*?
Do *clients* manipulate *designers*?
Do *designers* manipulate *design*?

Why do *designers* allow themselves to be manipulated?
Why do *designers* allow their work to be translated into money values?
Why can't *designers* be independent of *client*-fabricated trends?
Because the *client* provides their only means of subsistence from their work?

What does the *designer* want besides subsistence?
Is the *designer's* final goal money?
If not, what is it?
Love? Fame (i.e. temporary notoriety)? Immortality?

Does the *designer* care what anybody thinks about his work?
Does the *designer* care if anybody understands his work?
Who is the *designer's* public?
Other *designers*?
Critics? Curators? *Clients? Editors?*
Everybody else?

How much fame does a *designer* need? one year? ten years?
the top 10? the top 40?
How much fame can a *designer* take?
How much of a *designer* can fame take?
Is fame limited to *success*?
Is fame better than immortality?

Can immortality be a valid goal in *an age of global warming*?
Can immortality be bought? simulated?
What are the steps to immortality?
Studio–*website–blog–magazine–monograph–exhibition*?
Which of these steps are really necessary?
Is being in *exhibitions* enough for a *designer*?
Is being in *books* enough for a *designer*?
Are *design annuals* with *their* monetary basis a natural vehicle for design?

Do *designers* love their *clients* because they *pay their bills*?
Do *clients* love their *designers* or do they love the money they
make from *design* and *designers*?
Is *design* making love to oneself, to another, to others?

Is *design* a career (career="highway, a running from or to, carting, carrying")?
Is a career carousing?
Are *critics* pimps for carousing *designers* cruising immortality?

Are *critics* selling *design* or selling *designers*?
Are *clients* buying into *design* or buying into *designers*?
Are *clients commissioning design* or *commissioning commodities*?
Is *design* an investment? a social status symbol? decoration? fashion?

Are *designers* in *books* making *design* or commodities?
If there were no *clients* would *designers* make *design*?
Should *design look slick, hip,* or *timeless*?
Is *design* that's *slick commercial design*?
Is commercial *design good design*?
Does commercial *design* aspire to immortality?

Is *design* that's *very slick* better than other *design*?
Does it pay more because it's better than other *design*?
Should *design* be *compensated*? should *design* be *free*?
Should society support *designers* so they can give away their *services*?
Should all human beings support all human beings?

Should *design* be free?
Can *designers* be free?

"Offer them what they secretly want and they of course immediately become panic-stricken."

JACK KEROUAC, ON THE ROAD (1957)

FINDING DIAMONDS WITH DATAMINING

TOWARDS ECONOMIES OF DATA

Edial Dekker

Epistemologically speaking, information is made up of a collection of data while knowledge is made up of different strands of information. Today, the term 'data' and 'information' are increasingly difficult to tell apart.

Given enough raw data, today's algorithms and powerful computers can reveal new insights that would previously have remained hidden. Managed well, 'big data' can be used to unlock new sources of economic value, provide new insights into scions, and hold governments to account. But who is allowed to shape our cities, and how will they do it?
In the last decade, the development of digital networks and operations have produced an unprecedented wealth of information of aspects of urban life.[1] Adam Greenfield, Nokia's head of design direction for user interface and services, comments: 'We're able to interact with each other and with the urban environments around us when those environments have been provided with the ability to gather, process, and take action on data.'

Handheld electronics, location devices, telecommunications networks, and a wide assortment of tags and sensors are constantly producing a rich stream of data reflecting various aspects of urban life. Managed well, 'big data' can be used to unlock new sources of economic value, provide new insights into scions, and hold governments to account. Meanwhile, some of the world's foremost architects, planners, policymakers, builders, and thinkers are trying to understand this data to harness it for answers to our biggest problems.
In this article, I will address the new opportunities and inherent power that lie within these datasets and why it is necessary for everyone to participate. Health, crime rates, education, and the economy: almost every aspect of our lives is monitored and measured by the government. Traditionally, this data has widely been used to get a deeper understanding of behavioural patterns. It isn't new to derive patterns, spot trends, or identify outliers from data. But what is new, is the immense tsunami of new data that is available today and continues to grow. Thanks to advancements in sensing, networking, and data management, our society is producing data at an astonishing rate. According to one estimate, in 2010 alone we will generate 1,200 exabytes—60 million

times the content of the Library of Congress.[2] And some researchers predict that by the end of 2012, physical sensors will create 20 percent of non-video internet traffic.[3]

True opportunities in this novel development of seeing cities as an information architecture lie in the hands of its participants.[4] A question that comes to mind is: Who is allowed to shape our cities, and how will they do it? Unlike many other fields of design, cities aren't created by any one specialist or expert. There are many contributors to urban change, including ordinary citizens who can have a great impact on the perception of the cities in which they live, says Gary Hustwit, a documentary maker who has recently started to explore agency and urban life.

Having access to publicly available data creates a special kind of agency. Transportation systems, lighting systems, public media hardware like active signage and sound-systems will become objects available for activation, control, and coordination by tools and services that citizens use in their everyday lives. Through collaborative interaction with such tools, users of public spaces can configure them for specific temporary functions and even begin to 'perform' space together.[5] An example is 'Nuage Vert' a project which started in Helsinki whereby a laser beam illuminates the vapour emission of a coal burning CHP power plant, turning the smoke into a city scale neon sign. The green cloud then grows bigger in real time as local residents take control and consume less electricity.

From the above one can see that within the new petabytes of unexplored raw data that are available to anyone who is interested, lie many extremely valuable opportunities. 'What we are seeing is the ability to have economies form around the data - and that to me is the big change at a societal and even macroeconomic level,' says Craig Mundie, head of research and strategy at Microsoft. Which means data are becoming the new raw material of business and decision making: an input almost on a par with capital and labour. 'The data-centred economy is just nascent' concludes Mundie. And although large corporations will be hesitant to share data, more and more people are demanding open-data. A recent example happened in Iceland, where politicians and political activists are actively building an open-data network to regain trust and to show that their new politics have nothing to hide.

From better-informed government decision-making to easy tools to handle large quantities of data, the digital age is intimately interwoven with our daily lives. It's up to developers, designers, and citizens to bring their insight to the process of interpreting data and information and discover new ways to present them. Bearing in mind that visualisations — and the sparks they generate — will become more powerful when multiple people access them through collaborative rating and sense making.

1. SENSEable City Laboratory MIT, 2010. Senseable City Lab.
2. Heer, J., Bostock, M and Ogievetsky, V., 2010. A Tour through the Visualization Zoo.
3. Gartner, 2009. Gartner's Top 10 Predictions for 2009.
4. Coward, L.A. and Salingaros, N.A., 2005. The Information Architecture of Cities. Amsterdam: Techne Press.
5. Cervany, B., 2010. The Urbanode Project.

"Our battered suitcases were were piled on the side- walk again; we had longer ways to go. But no matter, the road is life."

JACK KEROUAC, ON THE ROAD (1957)

OPEN STANDARDS: DESIGN FOR ADAPTION

A NEW DESIGN VOCABULARY

Thomas Lommee

Whenever there was a need for sharing, open standards have always emerged as a means of generating more flexible and resilient models of exchange. Today, the pro-active consumer is no longer judging an object for what it is but rather imagines what it could become and the objects themselves are starting to behave more and more like dynamic puzzles, self-improving product versions rather than rigid monoliths.
Both producers and consumers are now enriching the overall product ecosystem by feeding it with new soft- and hardware plug-ins, updates and add-ons. Designing within certain common standards will, however, require a radically different mindset from all parties concerned.

Over the last 20 years we have been witnessing the early developments of a networked economy that is operated by its interconnected participants. Both companies and consumers have now potential access to a communication infrastructure that is geared towards sharing and exchange. This shift is profoundly changing our models of creation, production, and consumption.

Decentralised information streams and sources have altered people's attention scopes, ambitions, and goals and stimulated a more critical and pro-active attitude. Rather than swallowing manicured advertising made up by professional PR-departments, consumers are now informing, inspiring, and instructing each other with home-grown content - using twitters, blogs, and YouTube movies to communicate their skills, knowledge, and ideas. But the global mouth-to-mouth mechanism of the World Wide Web not only initiated a dialogue amongst consumers, it also started a conversation between consumers and producers. This emerging dialogue is generating exciting new business models and rearranging current artistic practices.

On the one hand it enables consumers to participate in the design process at various levels. Blogs facilitate product reviews and ratings and easy access to online instructions stimulate consumers to personalise, adapt, repair, or hack products. On the other hand, producers can now obtain a huge amount of feedback on their products by observing all these millions of small movements online and subsequently respond to them in their next product versions. Some producers are even actively involving the end-user in the creative process by asking them to design new applications (e.g. Apple's app store) or to propose new uses for their products (eg. roomba hoover).[1]

As a consequence, the consumer is developing a different, more active relationship with their products; the pro-active consumer is no longer judging an object for what it is but rather imagines what it could become and the objects themselves are starting to behave more and more like dynamic puzzles, self-improving product versions rather than rigid monoliths. Both producers and consumers are now enriching the overall 'product ecosystem' by feeding it with new soft- and hardware plug-ins, updates and add-ons. This shift from product to process allows the product to be adapted over time according to personal needs and flavours.

Out of this creative dialogue there is slowly emerging the need for a common design language, a kind of shared design vocabulary with its own specific rules, characteristics, and outcomes. This vocabulary is manifesting itself through common agreements within the dimensioning, assembly and material cycles of the object.

These agreements will facilitate collaborative design processes and stream-line customer interactions. Dimensional guidelines, through standardisation, will increase compatibility between interacting products. Design for disas-sembly, through self-evident construction and the use of reusable assembly techniques, will facilitate adaption and reparation. And finally, clear material certification will improve closed recollection and recycling processes.

The concept of introducing a set of open standards is nothing new. When-ever there was a need for sharing, open standards have always emerged as a means of generating more flexible and resilient models of exchange. The internet, for example, is entirely based on html coding, a common, free-of-charge text and image formatting language that allows everybody to create and share web pages and Wikipedia is nothing more than a common stand-ard template that can be filled in, duplicated, shared, and edited over and over again. We can clearly identify the use of open standards within our built environment as well. Our power infrastructure is a good example of a system that is regulated by specific design guidelines (standard plug diameters and bulb fittings), but also our logistical infrastructure is based on a set of com-mon agreements within the dimensioning of its individual components (from cardboard box to container ship). In all these examples it is no longer about one company that creates a complete system for all but rather about several companies who all contribute to a bigger, common system. But in order to do so they all have to operate within certain very specific, but mostly hidden, settings.

Despite the obvious advantages that these common standards and design protocols bring, there is considerable scepticism amongst designers to adopt and embrace them – probably because, until recently, a seemingly infinite amount of resources indicated little need for more flexible and open systems and mass communication offered few opportunities for exchange.[2]

In addition, these open models also raise questions around accountability, profitability, and formal expression. How do we credit the contributors, how do we generate money, and, last but not least, how do we balance openness and protection, freedom and restriction? Since every standard by definition imposes a restriction, it limits our choices and obstructs our freedom to design and shape and it disrupts our independent position as designers.

Nevertheless, the more we continue to share and exchange, the more the need for common platforms will surface within all aspects of our culture. This doesn't mean that one system will replace the other. Sometimes the commons will do a better job, other times the classical systems will prevail. Both open and closed systems will continue to exist, but it is the evolution of both in relation to the emergence of a networked society as well as the growing range of hybrids (closed systems with open components) that need to be closely observed and tried out.

Designing within certain common standards will require a different mindset from all stakeholders of the design process. In order to think 'within the box', in order to accept and embrace the new opportunities that emerge out of common restrictions, we need to acknowledge that we are part of a bigger whole, rather than being the whole itself. It requires us to give up the myth of creating 'something new', something that 'hasn't been done before' and to replace it by a willingness to dissolve into bigger projects that just make common sense. This new mindset will severely damage the romantic ideal of the 'designer-creator' and shift it towards the 'designer-collaborator'. And let's face it, that's quite a different perspective to work from, since no designer of our generation wants to be a pixel as we all want to be the full-colour image.

1. The Roomba is an autonomous robotic vacuum cleaner that comes with a serial interface. This interface is incompatible with standard PC/Mac serial ports and cables. It allows the user to monitor Roomba's many sensors and modify its behaviour. Programmers and roboticists create their own enhancements to Roomba resulting in numerous 'Roomba hacks'. Some hacks are functional, others are purely fun. Roombas have so far been converted into floor plotters, Wii remote controlled robots, 'hamster driven' vehicles etc.
2. Mass communication often results in a hierarchical, top-down monologue: one sender, mostly a company, state, or institution spreads a common message to the crowds through mass distribution channels like radio, TV, or printed media. This mode of communication offers few opportunities for the receivers to give feedback and limits their possibilities of discussing the content of message amongst each other. Peer-to-peer communication, on the other hand, generates a horizontal, decentralised dialogue : everybody informs everybody over the network. This allows all participants to swiftly exchange ideas, concepts, and designs.

"I woke up as the sun was reddening; and that was the one distinct time in my life, the strangest moment of all, when I didn't know who I was — I was far away from home, haunted and tired with travel, in a cheap hotel room I'd never seen, hearing the hiss of steam outside, and the creak of the old wood of the hotel, and footsteps upstairs, and all the sad sounds, and I looked at the cracked high ceiling and really didn't know who I was for about fifteen strange seconds."

JACK KEROUAC, ON THE ROAD (1957)

NEW DESIGNER'S APPLICATION FOR 2010–2020

THE INTERVIEW AS A NATURAL VACCINE

Annelys de Vet

CENTRE, 2010

Committee: On your CV we see that you were born in former Yugoslavia, grew up in Rwanda, and emigrated to Palestine; that you interned at an architectural firm there, then studied film for a few months in Baghdad, and recently graduated in Brussels with a degree in graphic design. With that background, what made you decide to become a designer?

New designer: During my life, I have experienced serious conflicts at first hand. My mother was a journalist, a war correspondent actually, so our family ended up in some strange situations, and I learned early on that it was impossible to get the experience of a place across in a nuanced way in the media. On the one hand, there was simply never enough time or space in the papers and news broadcasts; on the other, the international public seemed to lose interest quickly, even though there was no decrease in the intensity or tragedy of the conflicts. News only gets attention when it's literally new.

A key moment for me was when I realised that the media aren't merely a reflection of reality but are becoming more and more of a world of their own – one that has a terrifying influence, even a determining one, on current affairs, like political decisions and power structures. In Palestine I met several graphic designers who were exploring ways of using their profession to communicate their stories in different forms. I was very affected by that, because they were bringing together pleasure, optimism, and urgency. It showed how the practice of design could allow you to work at the cutting edge and reformulate what engages people.

After a brief and very instructive detour into film, I decided to study design, and by chance I ended up in Belgium. But since at the time I still thought of Brussels as a power hub, it seemed like a good observatory.

Your experience puts you ahead of a lot of designers – you can immediately put your insights into practice. Why do you want to continue studying?

If I am to stay standing in the face of the daily bombardment of information, I have to know precisely where I stand, who I am, and especially who else is talking. On the one hand, I feel that I need an autonomous position and an authentic voice to avoid going down in the bombardment; on the other hand, I'm noticing more and more lately that I can speak only in collaboration with other people and in relationship to other fields. I want to be able to establish alliances within constantly changing networks, to find the right tone, ask urgent questions, and combine forces with others. But I can't do it alone; I need an open institution where like minds gather, where I can have a critical sounding board, and where I can use design as dialogue. I need an environment that's not driven by economic principles and that gives space to the personal in relation to the public. I need an institute that functions as a think tank for visual strategies.

As you know, this institute offers an open curriculum in which you map out your own path. The institute believes in designers who take initiative, who speak out in a personal way, choose positions, and take responsibility. We seek to offer space to people who allow their own vision to drive their design choices and maintain a critical stance at all times toward the context and power structures they work in. Self-initiated projects are an implicit part of that. Can you tell us about the research project you hope to work on in the coming period?

My research will focus on the way in which media reporting influences the conditions we set for political freedom, democracy, and our collective morality. Mediagenic subjects often disproportionately dominate public debate, and I think that's part of what creates room for populist ideas and a rigid division between the self and the other. It makes me angry, but on the other hand, it creates new possibilities. I'd like to investigate how visual rhetoric – which graphic design in fact is – can be used to contribute to multivocality. How can we design processes that contribute to a more democratic culture? How can we use media networks to disseminate alternative images? What kinds of visual scenarios can we use to explicitly show the public nature of our culture expressly?

The ultimate form the results of this investigation will take is of course not yet definite, but I'm thinking along the lines of a fictitious interview, in which the form demonstrates its effectiveness as a natural vaccine against populism.

"I want to be like him.
He's never hung-up, he goes
every direction, he lets it all
out, he knows time, he has
nothing to do but rock back
and forth. Man, he's the end!
You see, if you go like him all
the time you'll finally get it."

JACK KEROUAC, ON THE ROAD (1957)

CITIZEN DESIGNER

21ST CENTURY ETHICS FOR GRAPHIC DESIGNERS

David Stairs

Assume nothing. Take only what you need.
Don't be greedy. And let me know if I was right next
century.

What does it mean to be a citizen designer anyway? Years ago Rick Poynor drew attention to it by defining it as 'a designer's relation to the public'. This seems self-evident, but is it half-enough? Are we talking about simple relations, or complex responsibilities? Is one's 'public' domestic or international? Is a designer more responsible to his neighbour, his society, or the community of all worldly life? And if the latter, can a designer be trusted to value non-human existence?

Are twenty first century ethics an improvement on nineteenth century ethics? Is sustainable design more significant than the antislavery movement? Are the Millennium Development Goals an attainable advance on colonialism? Are we really kinder and gentler than our forebears, or just more self-obsessed?

Can the current frenzy for socially conscious design counterbalance a century of design in the thrall of global capitalism? Does designing way-finding signs for refugee camps make more sense than Paul Rand at IBM, a Jewish designer working for a company complicit in the Holocaust? Can we peer through the haze of so much collective navel-gazing to be able to understand that design is not the Omphalos of the Universe? No discipline is a panacea for our earthly problems. It will take at least everyone working together before we can even consider 'saving the world'.

Wanting to frame these discussions in terms of knowing where we are going, one ought to remember where it is we've already been. One should not think narrowly. The universe is too broad. I used to believe that altruism was what was needed. Altruism is a modest start, but in itself it is not enough. Helping others is certainly part of a humane, moral, equitable practice, but only a part.

We need to actively engage the world with our whole focused intelligence, and it should not be avaricious. When I say this I don't mean it should necessarily be 'pro bono' either. Social design isn't free, as initiatives like design-NYC would have us believe. Designers need to shed their commercial skins though, and convince governments and societies that they are just as important as planners and politicians. Of course, actively entering civil society in an effort to protect the commons will be a novelty for most designers.

A designer who is a citizen of the twenty-first century must be a student of the past, an investigator of the present, and an imaginer of the future. Working to help the haves (those who can afford one's services) secure their dominance over the have-nots is no longer cool. Does this mean one has to dedicate one's life and career to striking a balance? This is impracticable, of course, though not a bad idea. At a minimum it means doing your homework and knowing for whom you're working.

Twenty first century ethics for Graphic Designers does not mean creating protest posters, or substituting websites for printed publications and calling this greener. By paying more attention to stakeholders than shareholders, tomorrow's designers might avoid the embarrassment of working to rebrand an acknowledged 'serial environmental criminal' like BP as Beyond Petroleum. But this takes more than merely knowing one's client or even one's world; it takes self-knowledge, probably the hardest type to acquire.

Designers, as a well-educated segment of society, have a stake, and can perhaps even take a lead in redefining professional practice as cooperative, civil, and just rather than competitive, corporate, and exploitative. This will seem alien at first. But once we are alien we will be standing with many of the others who are relegated to be on the outside looking in. Charles Eames always argued the value of changing one's perspective. Meanwhile, beware the prophets of global markets, global capital, and global communications, those purveyors of so-called 'massive change'. They will try to convince you of the value of their expertise. But the best things in life are not grand, the best things in life are small: a seed, a songbird, a child's hand. Not for nothing did Ghandi limit his worldly possessions to eyeglasses, a pen, a spinning wheel, and a bowl-and-spoon. For the rest of us it will be much more difficult. When you think you own the whole world, it isn't easy to take only a fair share.

What constitutes a fair share? A bicycle perhaps, rationed electricity, clean water, immunisations, a one-bedroom house, a publicly funded education, healthy food, socially beneficial work. With these things in hand, a citizen of the twenty-first century will be considered wealthy. With these things one should have no trouble finding one's heart's desire. With these few things a twenty first Century Designer could even change the world for the better.

So come along. Take a hand. Help out. We're all in this together. Assume nothing. Take only what you need. Don't be greedy. And let me know if I was right next century. If I'm wrong, chances are no one will remember. But I'm not wrong. Ethics is here to stay.

THE EXPANDING FIELD

GRAPHIC DESIGN 1900 - 2020

Mathias Augustyniak and Michael Amzalag founded M/M (Paris) back in 1992. They have worked together on many occasions with Dutch photographers Inez van Lamsweerde and Vinoodh Matadin. This sleeve for Björk's single 'Hidden Place' is one of the many results of them working as one creative force.

Courtesy: Wellhart Ltd/One One Little Indian

1899 | Ver Sacrum
Koloman Moser
magazine cover

2001 | Björk: Hidden Place
M/M (Paris), Van Lamsweerde & Matadin
record sleeve

Koloman Moser, together with Gustav Klimt and Josef Hoffmann, belonged to the Vienna Secession. This fin de siècle art collective elaborated on a localized approach to Art Nouveau. The magazine 'Ver Sacrum' played a pivotal role in binding the group and strengthening the development of their designs.

The academy award winning short film Logorama of French collective H5 zooms into a world consisting of Microsoft butterflies, Malibu palm trees and Pringle truck drivers. These and many other logos that populate our world have taken over and thus exemplify the absurdity of the amount of logotypes we are faced with in our daily lives.

1913 | Nunc est bibendum!!..
Marius Rossillon
poster

2009 | Logorama
H5 (F. Alaux, H. de Crécy & L. Houplain)
short film

Bibendum's plump disguise and enormous vitality make it hard to figure out his real age, but the Michelin Man, as he is commonly referred to, has been around almost an entire century. It started when the Michelin brothers suggested to cartoonist Marius Rossillon that he create a character from their own product. This subsequently turned into the Michelin man, which holds the dubious first position among corporate identities using a personification of a product.

Urban artist L'Atlas made his debut as a graffiti artist in the early 1990s in Paris. After graduating in art history, he went abroad to study classical Arabic calligraphy. Back in France L'Atlas started blending geometric Kufi scripts with the Latin alphabet and tagging the city with it using gaffer tape instead of the spray can.

1919 | Monogram for J.J.P. Oud
Theo van Doesburg
monogram

2008 | In girum imus nocte et consumimur igni
L'Atlas
wall design, Sète, France

Artist and writer Theo van Doesburg designed monograms for his friends the poet Antony Kok and the architect J.J.P. Oud. These monograms were executed on graph paper. The use of mathematical systems in art reflects the theory of Neo-Plasticism, a movement initiated by Van Doesburg and Mondriaan.

de COmputer mist de zintuigen en de middelen om zich uit te drukken de digitale wereld kent geen nuances in intonatie of emoties jelte van abbema zocht naar een manier om de virtuele wereld te vermenselijken een combinatie van virtueel en reeel verkent de grens tussen mens en machine deze tot tekstverwerker omgebouwde remington tiepemachine luistert hoe hard de toetsen worden aangeslagen bij een lichte aanslag wordt het font klein weergegeven terwijl er bij een harde aanslag grote letters op het scherm verschijnen

Designer Jelte van Abbema founded his Lab van Abbema to investigate how design, science, and technology can combine to shape a new landscape that reflects the contemporary nature of our world. His installation 'Virtureal' is an attempt to transfer emotions from writer to reader in a digital world. By incorporating touch sensitive sensors in an old Remington typewriter, emotional communication through a computer is recorded with each keystroke.

1921 | Boem Paukeslag
Paul van Ostaijen
typographic poem

2006 | Virtureal
Jelte van Abbema
expressive computer communication

BOEM

PAUKESLAG

PLAT

daar ligt alles

0_____o

weer nuwe violen celli bassen koperen triangel
trommels PAUKEN
razen rennen razen rennen razen RENNEN

STOP!

drama in volle slag hoeren slangen werpen zich op eerlike
mannen het gezin wankelt de fabriek wankelt
de eer wankelt ligt er
alle begrippen VALLEN

HALT!

This Dada poem by avant-garde poet Paul van Ostaijen (1896-1928) was created in the turbulent period after World War I. It was published in Bezette Stad (Occupied City), a bundle of typographic poems reflecting the author's feelings by the sight of the war wrecked city of Antwerp. Rhythmic typography was Van Ostaijen's attempt to bring unity in form and content.

Back in 2007, publicist Yosi Sergant suggested to Shepard Fairey that he create artwork in support of candidate Barack Obama. The initial poster based on a picture taken by Mannie Garcia featured the word 'progress'; this was later followed by versions with the words 'hope' and 'change'. Neither Yosi nor Shepard could have foreseen that this suggestion would result in an iconic image of the 2008 presidential election campaign that has already become legendary.

1922 | V Invest
unknown
poster

2008 | Barrack Hussein Obama
Shepard Fairey
poster

In the aftermath of World War I, the United States encouraged the public to participate in the extensive costs of the war by investing in war bonds, the so-called 'victory liberty loans'. This poster design is striking for its clarity and is somewhat unusual in a time where propaganda was mostly narrative.

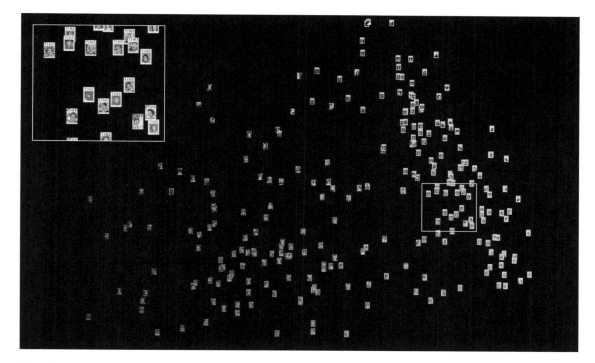

As professor of Visual Arts at the University of California and director of the Software Studies Initiative, Russian-born Lev Manovich is among the most influential thinkers in the field of new media and digital culture. This visualisation of his research shows people of colour that appeared on the cover of Time Magazine between 1923 and 2005.

1923 | Time Magazine unknown covers

2010 | Shaping Time Lev Manovich & Jeremy Douglass visualization

The covers of the first year editions of Time Magazine seen together could be interpreted as a visualisation of the 'Great Man Theory' that was highly popular in the 19th century. It was Herbert Spencer that countered this theory by saying that one could not attribute historical events to one person for he is a product of his social environment.

    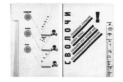

Berlin street artist Evol creates alienating views of the city by plastering his stencil posters of big grey building blocks and housing estates on city objects like power houses, switch-boxes, and walls. The series, called 'Plattenbauten', also includes paintings on cardboard which Evol places in public areas.

1923 | Metropolis
Paul Citroen
photo collage

2006 | Plattenbauten
Evol
stencil art

The quick expansion of cities at the beginning of the twentieth century prompted German-born Dutch artist and photographer Paul Citroen to make his best known collage 'Metropolis'. This vision of the future city, filled with skyscrapers, metros, and crowded streets, eventually inspired Fritz Lang to make his well known movie 'Metropolis' in 1927.

With their adaptation of the classic Argyle pattern for a pullover, graphic design collaborators Luna Maurer and Roel Wouters created a playful version of Op-Art. The distorted shape of the diamond pattern captures the tension between the daily use of a product and the ideals of traditional design.

1923 | Design for sports clothing
Varvara Stepanova
clothing designs

2004 | Argyle Pullover
Luna Maurer & Roel Wouters
clothing designs

These constructivist sports clothing designs by Varvara Stepanova were never produced, due to technical, political, and economical constraints at that time. Stepanova, wife of Alexander Rodchenko, was a talented artist and designer. Her sports designs were meant for everyday use and clearly convey the constructivist ideals of mathematical simplicity combined with aesthetic appeal.

The spectacular building for the Dutch Institute for Image and Sound (Media Park, Hilversum) designed by Neutelings Riedijk Architects, has a facade of coloured glass. Jaap Drupsteen took images from Dutch television heritage for the composition of these glass panels.

1924 | Design for a Newspaper Kiosk
Herbert Bayer
tempera & collage on paper

2006 | Netherlands Institute for Sound and Vision
Jaap Drupsteen
glass skin

While studying at the Bauhaus in Berlin, Austrian artist and architect Herbert Bayer made a design for a newspaper kiosk, in which the influences of De Stijl and Bauhaus are evident. The distinct use of lines and coloured surfaces, typical of the Bauhaus style, gain architectural relevance in this kiosk design, where sign becomes architecture.

Ever since Yves Saint Laurent drew his Mondriaan dress in 1965, designers of all kinds of consumer goods have been inspired by the Dutch painter's compositions in red, yellow, and blue. Piet Mondriaan the artist of the 1920s and 30s entered the urban scene of the 21st century with the Nike Dunk Low Pro SB.

1925 | Café De Unie, Rotterdam
J.J.P. Oud
gouache on paper

2004 | Nike Dunk Low Pro SB Mondriaan
Nike, Inc.
sneaker

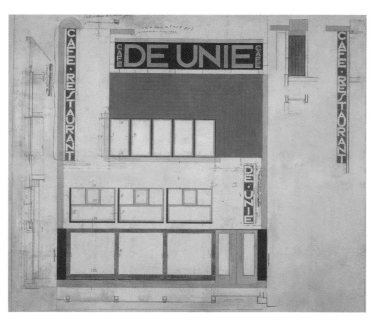

J.J.P. Oud's design for Café De Unie embodies the ideals of the movement De Stijl, with squares in primary colours and white. Originally meant to fill a vacant lot in the city for only ten years, the building was destroyed during the bombing of Rotterdam on May 14,1940. Architect Carel Weeber reproduced the current façade in 1986.

El Hema, an Arabic version of the typically Dutch warehouse HEMA, was invented to showcase the results of the Typographic Matchmaking project in which Dutch and Arabic typeface designers jointly designed new Arabic typefaces. These typefaces were integrated in the design of the pastiche store, that was made possible by Waël Morcos, Khajag Apelian, Maria Hakim, Raya Tueny & Abrar Al-Musallam.

1926 | Hema
unknown
store

2007 | El Hema
Mediamatic
design project

The HEMA opened its first shop in Amsterdam in 1926. The HEMA developed over the years into the favourite shop of all Dutch citizens by combining affordable prices with quality and good design. They are renowned for their annual design contest: the winning products can subsequently be bought in the shop.

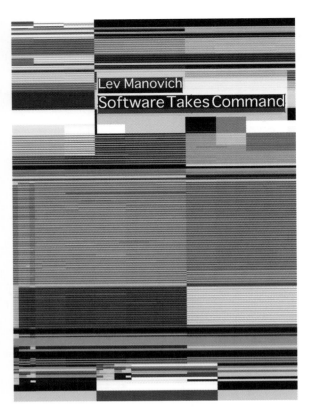

Lev Manovich
Software Takes Command

The fine lines and rhythmic patterns in this book cover by Dutch video artist and researcher Rosa Menkman, strongly reveal digital codes as part of the creation. The elusive force of the computerised is brought back into perspective by Menkman, for she focuses on error within the machine. Glitches form a pivotal role in her work.

1926 | Upward
Josef Albers
poster

2000 | Software takes command
Rosa Menkman
book cover

'Homage to a square, Upward, White Line Square 7' appear standard, somewhat course titles to abstract works. But German-born painter and designer Josef Albers investigated the relationships of colours in depth. After his training at Bauhaus, Albers moved to the United States, where he was a founding member of the American Abstracts Artists group.

       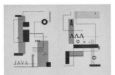

iFox
take back the web

When Apple introduced the iPod it once again revolutionised an entire industry. Apple's version of the MP3-player quickly became a must-have lifestyle accessory worldwide. Thus the iPod added to the carefully directed brand image of Apple, subsequently joined by the iPhone and the iPad.

1927 | Philips Radio
Louis Kalff
poster

2001 | iFox take back the web
unknown
parody

Trained as an architect, Louis Kalff started to work for Philips in 1925 as a designer of advertising and packaging for the company. When he left Philips in 1960 as artistic advisor to the board, Kalff had put his mark on Philips' image as an advanced and sophisticated electronics company.

American chocolate and confectionery manufacturer Hershey Foods marked the opening of its flagship store on Times Square in 2002 by unveiling this highlight in commercial shop branding: 65 x 18 meters of flashing, neon-lit chocolate bars and candies. Willy Wonka, eat your heart out!

1927 | Book Pavilion
Fortunato Depero
model of exhibition installation

2002 | Hershey's Chocolate Factory
Brian Collins
flagship store

The Book pavilion made for publisher Bestetti-Tum- minelli-Treves's presence at the 3rd International Exhibition of Decorative Arts in Monza is one of the better known works by Italian futurist Fortunato Depero. The advertising kiosk was built with typefaces reading 'libro' (book) and the publisher's name, thus symbolising the typographic process.

The Tokyo-based graphic collective Nam, founded by graphic designer Takayuki Nakazawa and photographer Hiroshi Manaka, currently numbers over ten artists from various backgrounds. Together they search for new possibilities in the world of visual arts. Their work, a blend of graphic design, photography, and other disciplines, is driven mainly by the collective's theme 'A fantasy in life'.

1928 | Die vier Grundrechnungsarten
El Lissitzky
silkscreen on paper

2008 | Bon Voyage (Kids Alphabet)
Nam
typeface

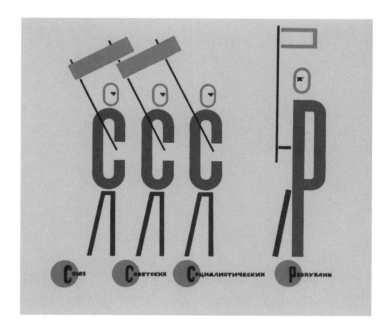

Trained as an engineer, El Lissitzky became an important influence on both the Dutch movement De Stijl and the artists of the German Bauhaus in the 1920s. Like Malevich, Lissitzky believed in a new art that rejected traditional pictorial structure. Visions of technology, mass production, and social transformation shaped his aesthetics.

The opening sequence for the television hit series Mad Men created by Imaginary Forces received the 2008 Emmy Award for outstanding title design. The design agency in Los Angeles and New York is known for its narrative solutions for film titles. The Emmy jury praised the graphic mini-story of a falling man for 'setting up the larger story that follows'.

Directors: Mark Gardner & Steve Fuller | Client: Lionsgate/AMC | Executive producer: Matthew Weiner

1929 | The Man with the Movie Camera
The Stenberg brothers
poster

2007 | Mad Men
Imaginary Forces
title sequence

The original poster for Dziga Vertov's movie 'The Man with the Movie Camera' is an example of mastery by the brothers Georgii and Vladimir Stenberg. When the Swedish-Russian brothers started to design their film posters in Russia during the early part of the 20th century, they had little or no precedents. Their constructivist images are characterised by dynamism and the combination of black and bold colours.

In most of his work, Portuguese artist Carlos No expresses a critical concern for disrespect of universal human rights. His exhibition 'Europe' was a critical comment on the issue of immigration, reacting to the approval by the European Parliament in 2008 of the so-called 'Return Directive'. Pictograms in traffic signs depict the true meaning of this European law.

1930 | Isotype / At Work
Gerd Arntz
visual language

2009 | Europe / Prohibited Traffic
Carlos No
traffic signs

Rooted in ideals of universal communication and emancipation of the (largely illiterate) proletariat, the more than 4,000 signs designed by Gerd Arntz for The International System Of Typographic Picture Education, developed by Otto Neurath, are the precursors of today's pictograms and infographics. Standardisation in the images allows for quick data interpretation, while small variations give the signs specific meaning.

The very popular campaign for the Dutch Socialist Party (SP) deployed an intelligent repertoire of design strategies, including viral ads with personal messages, resulting in 'a new form of media theatre in which the mass public in the audience is individualised' (Hugues Boekraad, GDM Magazine). A win-win situation, since the electorate received personal attention and the party gained recognition

1931 | Zuid-Holland Rood!
Meijer Bleekrode
regional election poster

2003 | SP (Dutch socialist party)
Thonik
identity & election campaigns

Founded in 1897, the Social Democratic Workers' Party (SDAP) initially strived for a socialist revolution by nationalising the means of production and by fostering a social security system. Eventually the party decided to improve the situation of Dutch workers through parliamentary means. Meijer Bleekrode was a graphic designer, lithographer, and painter who designed many powerful posters for the SDAP until he turned his back on politics in 1935.

SP.

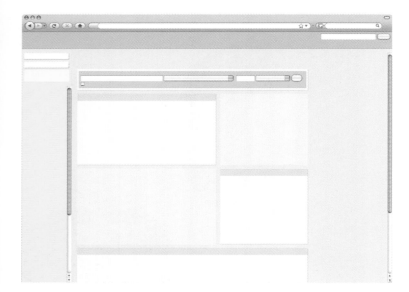

Editorial designer Hendrik-Jan Grievink is known for his visual culture criticism captured in popular and recognisable images. For 'Template Culture' he stripped well-known websites - in this image Marktplaats.nl - of their content, reshaping them into mere aesthetic objects. The result is an alienating view on the standards used in web design today.

1932 | Typographische Entwurfstechnik
Jan Tschichold
book

2003 | Template Culture
Hendrik-Jan Grievink
visual commentary

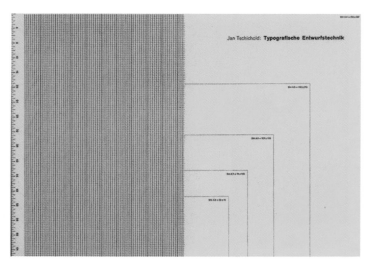

In his manifesto on modernist design Die Neue Typographie (1928), typographer and book designer Jan Tschichold laid out polemical rules for a well designed printed page. Tschichold put clarity above all else and advocated the use of standards. His subsequent Typographische Entwurftechnik elaborated on how to draw layouts.

The rules for designing 3D letters are completely different than the rules for lettering that traditionally has to survive in ink on paper or nowadays on screen. The letters for this fire basket are conical and there are no curves involved. The 24 one-word poems written by Knip relate in a more autonomous way to fire.

1933 | Campari Pavilion
Fortunato Depero
model

2001 | Fire Basket
gebr.Knip
steel, lasercutting

Italian futurist artist Furtunato Depero, originally a marble worker who grew up in Rovereto where his Casa d'Arte Futurista can still be visited, designed many outings for the alcoholic beverage company Campari. His design for a Campari pavilion was one in a series of typographic advertising kiosks.

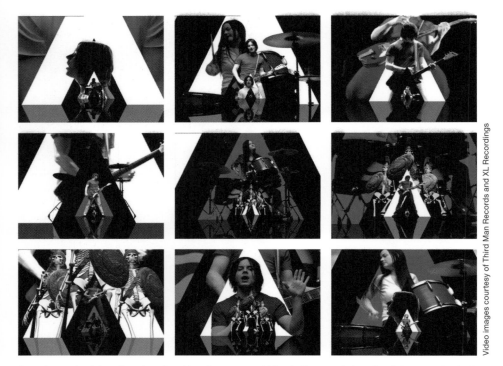

French music video directing duo Alex Courtes and Martin Fougerol visualised the award-winning rock song 'Seven Nation Army' by The White Stripes in a kaleidoscopic video clip that by its repetitive nature never seems to stop.

1940 | The Men Are Ready...
unknown
poster

2009 | 'Seven Nation Army' by The White Stripes
Alex Courtes and Martin Fougerol
music video

THE MEN ARE READY...

ONLY **YOU** CAN GIVE THEM WINGS

An endless line of pilots awaiting planes still to be paid for by the public has become a classic Canadian image related to World War II. It has all the features of a wartime propaganda poster, skillfully using the strong argument of repetition.

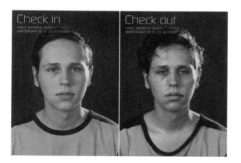

Cheap has its price, so Amsterdam-based advertising agency KesselsKramer advised Hans Brinker Budget Hotel in 1996 to be proud of its lousy reputation. The anti-campaign promoting the dog shit in front of the entrance and lice in every bed, became famous throughout the world. Thirteen years of imagery for the campaign was bundled in the book 'The Worst Hotel In The World'.

1940 | Pitto is best
Pieter den Besten
advertisement

2009 | The worst hotel in the world
KesselsKramer
book for Hans Brinker Budget Hotel

During World War II, Rotterdam-based coffee and tea company Van Nelle was forced to switch to surrogate coffee. Artist and graphic designer Pieter den Besten, who made many advertisements for the company, couldn't do much more than simply state that Van Nelle's Pitto was among the best available.

      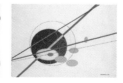

This stop-motion of UK-based directing collective Tell No One (Remi Weekes and Luke White) is a digital victory over collage. The final still of this short reminds us of the dancing series of Dégas, where the spectator remains distant like a voyeur.

1940 | Clean Packages Instead of Dirty Hands
Herbert Matter
advertisement

2010 | Seaweed
Tell No One
lo-fi video experiment

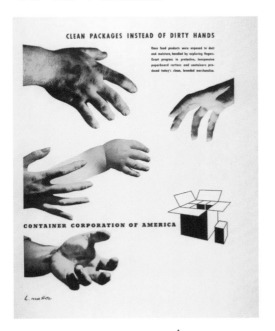

Herbert Matter was an avant-garde artist before he dedicated himself to the craft of graphic design in 1929. Trained among masters such as Fernand Léger, Cassandre and Le Corbusier, he creatively mixed photographic skills with delicate typography. His fascination for collage and the revolutionary 'photogram' are clearly visible in this advertisement for Container Corporation of America.

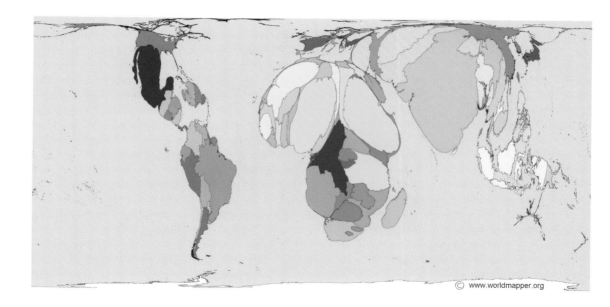

Using a method developed by physicists Michael T. Gastner and M. E. J. Newman, geography researchers Dorling and Hennig from the SASI Research Group of the University of Sheffield created hundreds of cartograms, distorted maps showing each country in proportion to a specific topic.

1940 | The world according to Standard (N.J.)
Richard Edes Harrison
information visualization

2010 | Worldmapper
Danny Dorling, Benjamin David Hennig
cartography

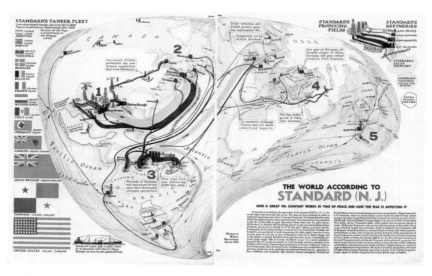

Freelance cartographer Richard Edes Harrison was admired for the innovative and imaginative maps he published during the 1930s and 1940s in different magazines. This map accompanied a series of three articles in Fortune on the Standard Oil Company of New Jersey.

The impact of design when creating an identity has cleverly been reversed engineered by Greenpeace's campaign Behind The Logo against a global oil and gas company. In this campaign, Greenpeace invited people worldwide to rework the existing logo. The winning graphic by Laurent Concours had the grim appearance of a cormorant bird, dripping in oil against the yellow and green BP sunflower.

1941 | Labor
Joseph Binder
poster

2000 | Behind the Logo
Greenpeace
competition

At the peak of graphic modernism, Austrian-born American designer Joseph Binder, reduced geometric form in his designs and moved against the tide. His primary passion for painting and his fascination for the psychological dimension of colour, strengthen this 1941 poster design. His work has been of great importance to the 20th century visual heritage of the United States.

When the designers who together form Gorilla presented their graphic comment panel on the front page of Dutch national newspaper De Volkskrant in 2006, they surprised the world with a new form of social commitment by design. After being awarded various design prizes, the graphic columns were bundled in the book 'The Daily Gorilla'.

1947 | Herstel gehavend Nederland door arbeid
Wim Brusse
poster

2000 | The Daily Gorilla
De Designpolitie
book

Graphic designer Wim Brusse started his career as the assistent of designer Paul Schuitema. Brusse's book covers with photo collages reveal the influence of his teacher. As a former member of the resistance during WO II, Brusse used his skills after the war to help rebuild the battered country.

Photo: urban_data

Evan Roth, James Powderly and Theo Watson from Graffiti Research Lab created L.A.S.E.R. Tag. In its simplest form the Laser Tag system is a camera and laptop setup, tracking a green laser point across the face of a building and generating graphics based on the laser's position which then get projected back onto the building with a high power projector. Resulting in a true "weapon of mass defacement".

1949 | Picasso Uses Light Pen
Pablo Picasso, Gjon Mili
photo

2007 | L.A.S.E.R. Tag
Graffiti Research Lab
laser, open source software, projector

When photographer Gjon Mili, a technical genius and lighting innovator working for Life magazine, visited Pablo Picasso he showed him some of his photographs of ice skaters with tiny lights affixed to their skates. The pictures incited Picasso to make a series of light drawings using a small flashlight in a dark room, that Mili was able to catch on film.

Under the name of Raw Color, designers Christoph Brach and Daniera ter Haar study the powerful colours of vegetables. For their installation '100%JUICE', vegetables were transformed to a natural ink used to feed a new printing process. This process, leading the ink through the paper, enabled the viewers to see the poster print slightly grow.

1949 | Joy
Cornelius van Velsen
advertisement

2007 | 100% JUICE
Raw Color
installation

In postwar Netherlands, poster designer Cornelius van Velsen was much in demand for the design of commercial posters. A versatile craftsman, Van Velsen generally worked on intuition, always searching for images that would appeal to the public. Like his well-known posters for Dutch lemonade drink Joy, made from real fruit.

Since 1989 American-French designer Pippo Lionni has been using well-known pictograms to criticise society in a satirical way. Eight recent pieces of his Re-animation series were screened on a 40 square meter urban screen at Contemporary Art Screen Zuidas (Amsterdam), giving new meaning to public service announcements.

1952 | Schützt das Kind!
Josef Müller-Brockmann
poster

2009 | Rape (Part of Re-Animation series)
Pippo Lionni
installation animation

This poster 'Schützt Das Kind!' ('Watch That Child!') was the first poster from the public health and safety poster series designed using the photomontage technique. These series, sponsored by the Swiss Automobile Club, were intended to warn drivers on the dangers of speeding.

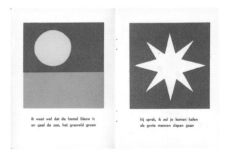

Dick Bruna's iconic visual language was taken as the starting point for the 10th anniversary edition of the biennial books that present the work of members of the Dutch designers association BNO. For the book, Bruna worked together with one of the leading design agencies in the Netherlands today, De Designpolitie.

1953 | The apple
Dick Bruna
book

2008 | My Dutch Design
De Designpolitie, Dick Bruna
book

Dick Bruna came from a publisher family and at the age of 26 designed his first illustrated children's book about an apple. The simple designs in clear colours prelude his series about a little rabbit called Miffy (Nijntje), which is now famous throughout the world. Bruna's drawing style has become iconic and captivates the imagination of millions all over the globe.

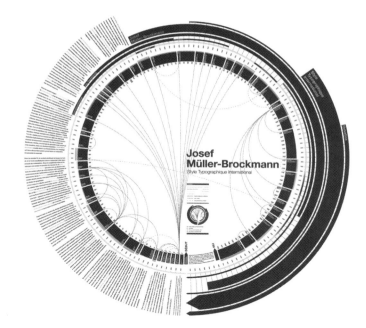

A personal web research on Josef Müller-Brockmann resulted in a data visualisation, called 'Josef Müller-Brockmann and the International Style', containing three key elements: the research of information on the web, chronological information on Müller-Brockmann's life and work, and a critical article based on the information found.

1955 | Beethoven
Josef Müller-Brockmann
poster

2008 | Josef Müller-Brockmann
Quentin Delobel
poster

Although Müller-Brockmann took a strict constructive approach to the Beethoven poster he made on assignment from the Zurich Tonhalle, he was able to retain a sense of musicality in the design. This poster was one of a series of concert posters that evoke the idea of music in structured designs.

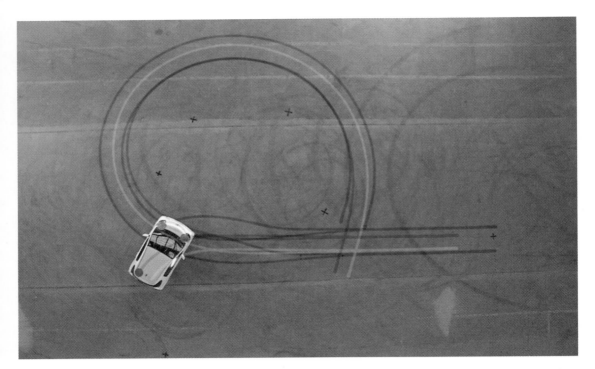

An overhead camera in a hangar, specially made software, a small white car with four coloured dots op top, and a professional racing driver. That was all the Belgian-French graphic design agency Pleaseletmedesign needed to create the IQ Font for Toyota.

1957 | Scooter Pirelli
Max Huber
advertisement

2009 | IQ Font
Pleaseletmedesign
the making of IQ Font for Toyota

Tyre manufacturer Pirelli was known for commissioning many innovative designers for their advertising. Swiss-born designer Max Huber was at the height of his career when he made this poster that is reminiscent of his legendary Monza Race posters. Huber was also famous at the time for his jazz record covers and music magazine designs.

COEXISTENCE

The symbolic message promoting the peaceful coexistence of religions was made by Polish graphic designer Piotr Mlodozeniac for a contest sponsored by The Museum on the Seam for Dialogue, Understanding, and Coexistence in Jerusalem. Ironically the sign itself caused conflicts regarding the ownership involving different parties interested in selling T-shirts, posters, and other articles bearing adaptations of the sign.

1958 | Campaign for Nuclear Disarmament
Gerald Holtom
logo

2001 | Coexist
Piotr Mlodozeniac
design

In 1958, in the midst of the Cold War, designer Gerald Herbert Holtom designed the logo of the British Campaign for Nuclear Disarmament. The position of the lines within the circle was based on combining the semaphore signals for the letters N and D. Eventually the sign evolved into a worldwide symbol for peace.

Asked to design a poster to promote Gary Hustwit's homage to the classic Helvetica typeface designed in 1957 by Swiss designers Max Miedinger and Eduard Hoffmann, Amsterdam design agency Experimental Jetset came up with this poster, presenting the type characters as the cast. They also appeared in the film themselves.

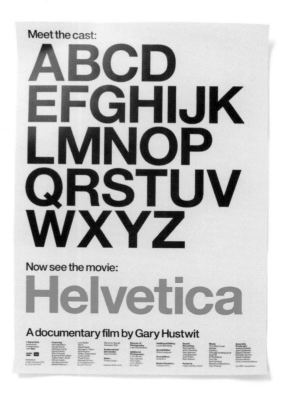

1959 | Watching Words Move
I. Chermayeff, T. Geismar, & R. Brownjoh
experimental typography

2006 | Meet the Cast
Experimental Jetset
poster for Gary Hustwit / Plexifilm

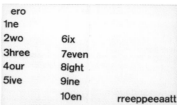

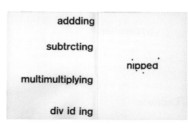

In their booklet called 'Watching Words Move', designers Ivan Chermayeff, Tom Geismar, and Robert Brownjohn playfully expressed that type itself could speak, even when they used a rigid type like Helvetica, which was then just 5 years old. They showed that a suggestion of movement and narrative could be created by the placement of letters and the choice of symbols.

The attraction of everything small gave shape to this miniature catalogue by designer Irma Boom. Boom thoroughly loves books as objects, and dedicates her life to making them. Structure and tangibility are essentials in the creation of her books, and miniature dummies are proof of their magic.

1959 | Think Small
William Bernbach
advertisement

2010 | Irma Boom: Biography in Books
Irma Boom
catalogue

Courtesy: Volkswagen AG

In the late 1950s Paul Rand developed the 'The Big Idea' concept. In this innovating approach to advertisement, with an educational undercurrent, the visual became as important as the copy. This approach activates another part of the brain and provokes a certain visual intelligence in the spectator. Here, advertising icon Bill Bernbach translated 'The Big Idea' into a real advertisement.

In an ultimate attempt to emancipate his distinctive sides, this little man is tearing himself apart. Elegant, balanced, and handsome with his typeface Pacific Standard, or ingenious and clumsy with his Bebedot Blonde, Kisman always shines in versatility. Because of this, neither this work nor any other in particular can define his entire oeuvre that deserves to be investigated thoroughly.

1959 | Anatomy of a Murder
Saul Bass
film poster

2006 | De Tweedeling van België
Max Kisman
illustration

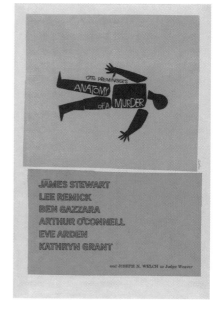

Groundbreaking and multi-facetted graphic designer Saul Bass is mainly known for his cinematic work. He designed film posters for the likes of Billy Wilder and Alfred Hitchcock and these have since become part of our collectively shared visual data-bank. By applying kinetic typography in title sequences, Bass moved the standard and presence of credits in film. Bass wanted designs to make people feel as well as think.

In a Flickr image set, djgeek collects default profile pictures used in social media by participants who do not or do not want to upload a profile picture of their own. A fascination for the 'default' image shared by many users resulted in this growing collection of how the people behind social media fill in the blanks.

1960 | Ionesco | Stolarna
John Melin, Anders Österlin
poster

2010 | default profile pictures
djgeek
image collection

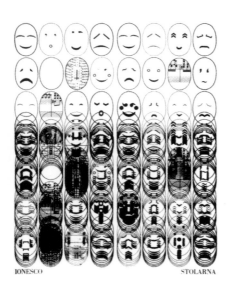

IONESCO   STOLARNA

Ionesco's play The Chairs (1952) is about two characters preparing chairs for a series of invisible guests, implicitly standing for everyone in the world, gathering for a revelation (as it is implied) about the meaning of life. In their poster for the play, Swedish advertising duo John Melin and Anders Österlin gave the invisible crowd a face.

For an exhibition commemorating the 50th anniversary of the Helvetica typeface in London's Design Museum, 50 designers were asked to make a 50 x 50 cm poster linked to one specific year. For 1966 the independent Amsterdam graphic design studio Experimental Jetset took Antonioni's masterpiece 'Blow-Up' as a starting point for their contribution.

1961 | Letzes Jahr in Marienbad
Hans Hillmann
poster

2007 | Blow-up
Experimental Jetset
poster for Mark Blamire / Blanka

From 1953 onwards, when he started his own studio in Kassel, German graphic designer Hans Hillmann designed numerous movie posters for the institute for artistic cinema Neue Filmkunst. Hillmann was a master in capturing the essence of a movie in an image, thus influencing generations of designers after him.

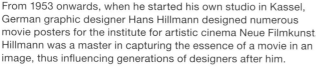

eBoy designers Kai Vermehr, Steffen Sauerteig, and Svend Smital are masters of Pixel Art. By blowing up and editing on pixel level, they create colourful digital imagery with a surprisingly authentic feel. By moving away from the perfectionist claim of digital progress, eBoy stresses the impediment of creating images, stripping bare the basic elements of construction.

1961 | Vivaldi Gloria
Rudolph de Harak
record cover

2008 | Tokyo City
eBoy
poster

Courtesy: Deutsche Grammophon

With his bright and playful use of colour, California-born graphic designer Rudolph de Harak moves his creations one step away from classical modernist structures. De Harak created a vast body of work during the 1960s, ranging from magazine illustrations and exhibition designs to book covers, all of which convey a highly experimental and human approach.

Ben er weer

Ben bereikbaar via www.ben.nl

KesselsKramer invented Ben, both a Dutch boy's name and the Dutch translation of the first person singular of the verb 'to be', as the brand name for a Dutch mobile network. The campaign shows that the network is intended for everyone, while at the same time depicting the multi-coloured face of today's society.

1961
You don't have to be Jewish to love Levy's
Bill Bernbach & Howard Zieff
campaign for Levy's

2005
Ben er weer
KesselsKramer
campaign for Ben (Dutch phone company)

You don't have to be Jewish to love Levy's
real Jewish Rye

For a small family-owned bakery in Brooklyn, American ad agency Doyle Dane Bernbach (DDB) made one of the most memorable print ad campaigns of all time. Depicting ordinary New Yorkers from all backgrounds in happy portraits by photographer Howard Zieff, the campaign did more than simply promote rye bread.

With his Italic shaped poster, Berlin-based graphic designer Eivind Molvær questions the modernist cult of standardisation and moves the rules of good graphic design to another level. The democratic principles that underline Tschichold's standards of design, with its DIN-sizes and economic ideals, are humourously and effectively attacked: How to print an italic poster?

Photography: Sven Ellingen

1961 | Typographische monatsblätter
Emil Ruder
magazine cover

2007 | The Italic Poster
Eivind Molvær
poster

Emil Ruder, co-founder of the Basel School of Design, played a key function in the development of the so-called Swiss style that builds on Jan Tschichold's 'new typography'. This movement aims to capture the elements of modern life through form. Asymmetry, geometric patterns, and logic provided a typographic message with a dynamic feel.

Photography: www.thisisdisplay.org

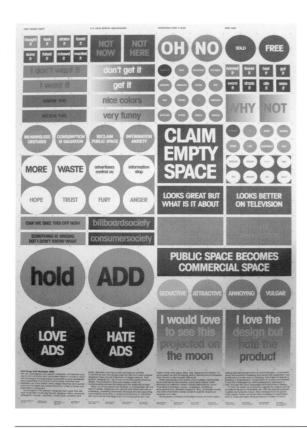

In 2000, 33 visual communicators decided to renew the 1964 manifesto of 22 designers calling for their skills to be put to worthwhile use. 'We propose a reversal of priorities in favour of more useful, lasting, and democratic forms of communication', the new manifesto read. Two of the undersigned, Armand Mevis and Linda van Deursen, made a visual translation.

1964 | First Things First Manifesto
Ken Garland
poster

2000 | First Things First Manifesto 2000
Mevis & Van Deursen
poster

British designer Ken Garland wrote and proclaimed his famous manifesto against the predominance of commercial advertising during a crowded meeting of the Society of Industrial Artists on 29 November 1963. Many attendees immediately volunteered their signatures and when the manifesto was published in January 1964, designers from all over the world expressed their sympathy.

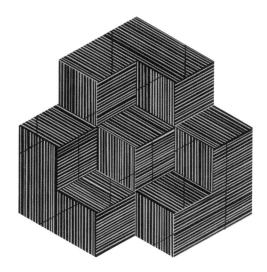

Toronto-based Way Shape Form is a design partnership between Matthew Boyd and River Jukes-Hudson. The designers took part in the creation of the collaborative zine Totally Rad, a 76-pages magazine with contributions from 32 artists, published in a limited edition of 200 hand-numbered copies. This is one of their contributions.

1964 | Woolmark
Francesco Saroglia
certification mark

2008 | Totally Rad
Way Shape Form
design

The Woolmark logo, designed by Italian designer Francesco Saroglia for the Australian International Wool Secretariat as a certification mark for pure woolen fabrics, was launched in 1964 in Britain, the US, Japan, Germany, Holland, and Belgium. In 1997, the IWS changed its name to The Woolmark Company.

During the month of Ramadan in 2001, the artists Tarik Sadouma and Bastiaan Franken turned a former supermarket in Amsterdam into a mosque, decorated with artwork from that used by the grocery chain. Five times a day people came in to pray, kneeling towards the name of Allah made out of the Albert Heijn logo.

1965 | Albert Heijn Supermarket
James Pilditch
logo

2001 | Albert Heijn Mosque
Bastiaan Franken & Tarik Sadouma
installation

The logo design for the leading Dutch supermarket chain Albert Heijn was designed by James Pilditch, founder of packaging design agency Allied International Designers (AID). Half a century after its introduction, the logo has become an intrinsic part of Dutch culture and is probably one of the most famous logos in the Netherlands.

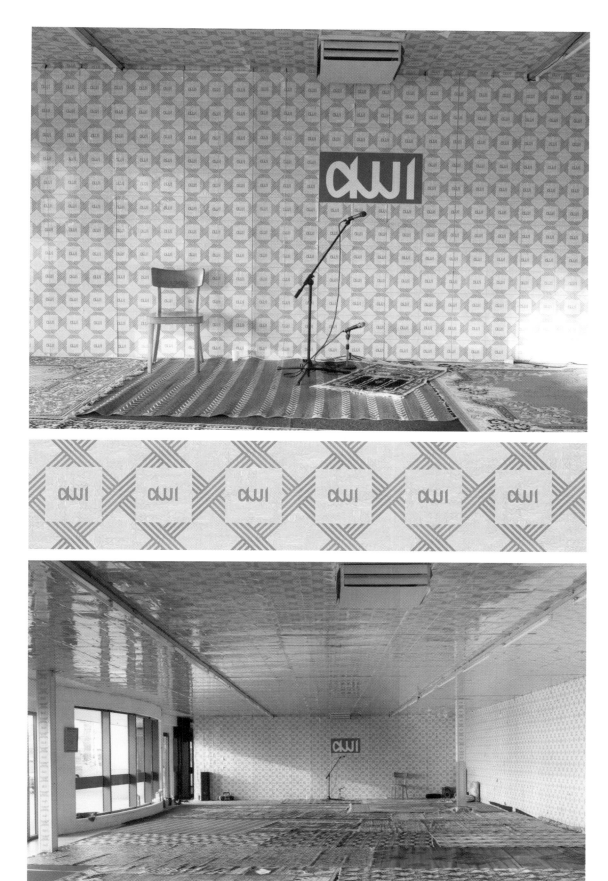

SNCF's 70th anniversary slogan 'Donner au train des idées d'avance' was visualised in a way characteristic for Richard Niessen and Esther de Vries. It shows the influence of Italian designers like Sottsass in an approach that is both systematic and exuberant. Niessen & De Vries seek longevity in their designs through richness in layers.

1965 | Olivetti
Enzo Mari
poster

2008 | 70th anniversary French Railway SNCF
Niessen & De Vries
poster

As a writer, teacher, artist, and designer of products, furniture, and puzzle games, Italian Enzo Mari has been influential on both his peers and younger generations in the worlds of design and culture. He was a founding member of the radical artistic movement Nuova Tendenza and taught at many universities in Italy and Europe.

Participation is key in this 2010 video clip for C'mon & Kypski, produced by Vincent Lindeboom. As co-authors of the 'Conditional Design Manifesto' Puckey and Wouters aim to work in the here and now. The process is the product; the designers strive to create by merely defining the constraints or as in this case the choreography (Sabine Linz).

1966 | Screen Tests
Andy Warhol
short films

2010 | One Frame of Fame
Jonathan Puckey & Roel Wouters
video clip

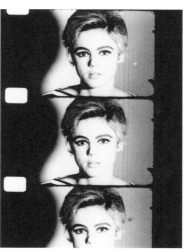

Andy Warhol's Screen Tests were filmed from early 1964 to November 1966. Today, everyday is a screen test, and everybody stars in their own film. Only half aware of the implications, we gladly submerge ourselves in a world dominated by social networking, cameras, and media devices. It has become hard to escape the 15 minutes. We now are our own stars, and our own audience.

One of the first typographic experiments of Utrecht based design agency Autobahn was Tapewriter. A font made with the use of an iron fence and a roll of duct tape. The typeface allows anyone in possession of a roll of tape, to submit his or her message to the world in a clear and sophisticated manner.

1967 | New Alphabet
Wim Crouwel
typeface

2005 | Tapewriter
Autobahn
typeface

Dutch graphic designer and modernist Wim Crouwel designed his 'New Alphabet' out of dissatisfaction with the quality of early photographic typesetting machines, while foreseeing a more digitised future for the graphic profession. This typeface, which was intended to start a professional discussion, was better adopted to the vertical movements of the cathode ray tube in the first typesetting machines.

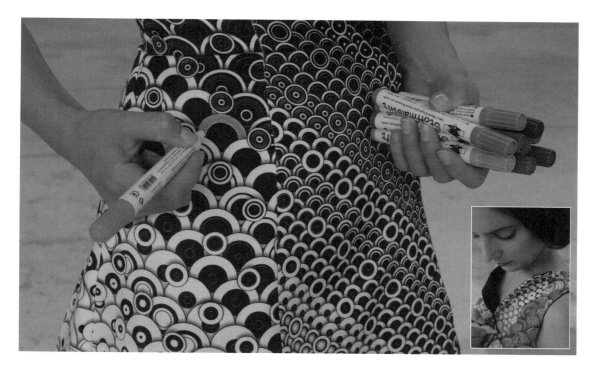

Berber Soepboer & Michiel Schuurman have integrated DIY culture into fashion. The loud shapes in dazzling patterns, photographed by Sander Marsman, pay tribute to the iconic graphic imagery of the 1960s. Whoever wears this dress, in this case model Nina Varga (styled by Anne Stooker), is guaranteed uniqueness.

1967 | Bob Dylan
Milton Glaser
poster

2008 | Colour-In dress
Berber Soepboer & Michiel Schuurman
clothing

New York-born graphic designer Milton Glaser is considered one of the most influential designers of our time. His playful, yet highly conceptualised approach to design, resulted in a broad range of strong images. With Bob Dylan's colourful curls, Glaser managed to reflect perfectly the psychedelic spirit of the late sixties music scene.

In the installation Flyers, New York graphic designer Yeju Choi played with the medium of printed flyers. When the originally uniform 2D flyers are put up on billboards, they become constantly changing 3D objects. Choi cut up pictures of these flyers and turned them into new flyers, put them back on the site, and photographed them again.

1967 | New Darmstadt Secession Exhibition
Helmut Lortz
exhibition poster

2007 | Flyers
Yeju Choi
Installation

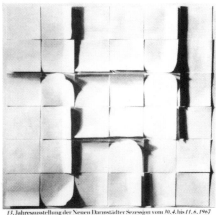

13. Jahresausstellung der Neuen Darmstädter Sezession vom 30.4. bis 11.6.1967
Darmstadt Ausstellungsgebäude Mathildenhöhe ■ Öffnungszeiten:

Graphic artist and craftsman Helmut Lortz was educated at a crafts school for ivory and woodcutting in Erbach, Germany. In 1948 he joined the Neuen Darmstädter Sezession (New Darmstadt Secession) and in 1954 the designer of numerous book covers, illustrations, posters, and logos was the first German to join the Alliance Graphique Internationale.

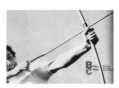

For the opening of their exhibition at Deitch Projects in New York, Sagmeister (art-direction), Richard The (design), and Joe Shouldice (design) produced a wall made of 10,000 bananas. Green bananas created a pattern against a background of yellow bananas spelling out the phrase: Self-confidence produces fine results. After a number of days the green bananas also turned yellow and the words disappeared.

1967
The Velvet Underground & Nico
Andy Warhol
album cover

2008
Banana wall
Stefan Sagmeister
exhibition at Deitch Projects, NY

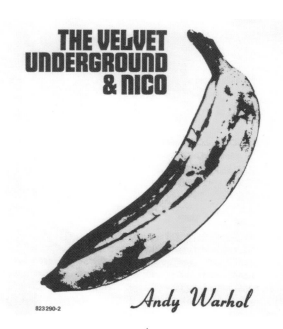

The debut album of the legendary rock band The Velvet Underground with singer Nico was delayed because of the banana on its cover. Pop artist Andy Warhol wanted the banana skin to be a sticker which could be peeled back to reveal a flesh-coloured banana underneath. Production of this took extra time and costs, and today an intact cover is a rare collector's item.

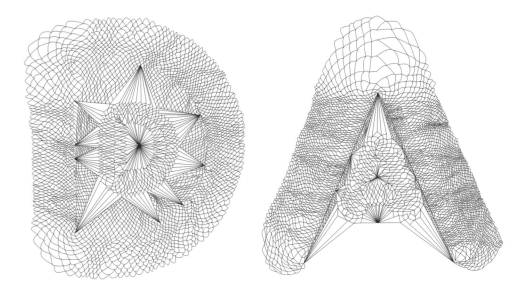

Halfway through her studies, Hansje van Halem started drawing letters with the use of a mouse pen. This enabled the Amsterdam-based graphic designer to overcome the distance between her and the computer and to make her handwork digital. By filling letter forms with lines, Van Halem manipulates the grey tones at will, creating almost hallucinating patterns.

1967 | Mister Tambourine Man
Martin Sharp
screenprint

2008 | Wire Type
Hansje van Halem
typeface sketches

Thea Proctor Memorial Fund 1970 | Collection: Art Gallery of New South Wales
© Martin Sharp

Psychedelic posters for such musicians as Bob Dylan, Donovan, and Jimi Hendrix brought Australian artist Martin Sharp fame as one of the foremost pop artists in the world. His archetypal 'Blowing in the Mind / Mister Tambourine Man' poster is a two-colour screenprint, red and black ink on gold reflective foil paper.

Photography: Maurice Boyer

When designing the identity for Rotterdam museum Boijmans van Beuningen, Thonik used 'Mexcellent' as his starting point. As with the design for the 1968 Olympics, the Amsterdam agency chose to emphasise the type by elongating it into the entire visual. Thonik, though, took the psychedelics back to the grid, revealing a contemporary version of the international style. In Thonik's design the Central American aspect has given way to a more Calvinist geometrics.

1968 | Mexico City Olympic Games
L. Wyman, P. Ramirez Vazquez, E.Terrezas
poster

2008 | Museum Boijmans van Beuningen
Thonik
identity and visual communication

The refreshing graphic psychedelics of the emblematic style of the 1968 Olympics include a convincing mix of Op-Art and native Huichol art. After the games, this logo design by Eduardo Terrezas, Pedro Ramirez Vasquez, and Lance Wyman, was reworked into the font Mexcellent.

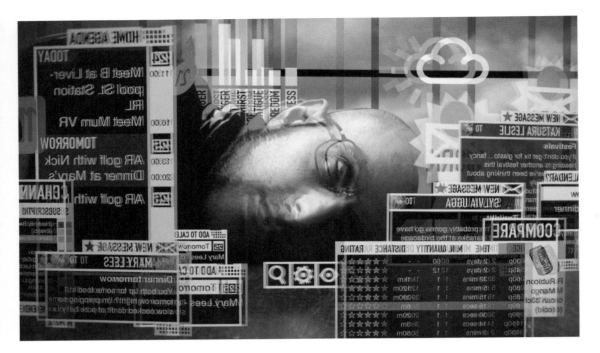

Keiichi Matsuda began working with video as a critical tool to understand, construct, and represent space. His multi-disciplinary research explores the social/spatial implications of emerging technologies for the city, focusing on the integration of media into everyday life. This short film is part of 'Augmented (hyper)Reality', a larger project about the social and architectural consequences of new media and augmented reality.

1969 | Bauhaus
Muriel Cooper
book for MIT Press

2010 | Augmented City
Keiichi Matsuda
short film

Muriel Cooper was a true pioneer of a new design area, one of the first graphic designers to explore deeply the possibilities of electronic media and possibilities such as 3-D text. She clearly understood that the digital world brought with it a whole range of issues and problems, and she was determined to understand these properly.

Singapore-based designer collective fFurious efficiently makes use of the cult status of a world famous lollipop by deconstructing its features in this 'designer toy'. Trexi is a company that provides in canvas art toys that can be personalised in a variety of styles by different designers and artists. This vinyl toy is part of the Trexi Series 02 worldwide release.

1969 | Chupa Chups
Salvador Dali
logo

2010 | Trexi Chap | Play Imaginative
fFurious
toy customisation

It might be surprising for some to learn that the Chupa Chups logo was designed by Spanish surrealist Salvador Dali.

Over the course of several months beginning October 2008 to April 2009 Rhett Dashwood spent some of his spare time between commercial projects searching Google Maps hoping to discover land formations or buildings resembling letter forms.

1970 | Naked ladies alphabet
Anton Beeke
typeface

2008 | Google Maps Typography
Rhett Dashwood
landscape

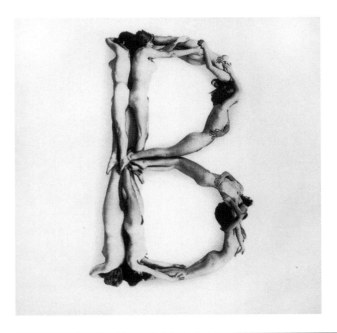

Anthon Beeke's 'Naked ladies alphabet', made for the famous Kwadraatbladen series of printer Steendrukkerij de Jong & Co., was a reaction on Wim Crouwel's New alphabet, presented three years before in the same series. As Beeke said: 'Crouwel was the beginning of a new era and I closed the history that started in 1168 with a monk who created an illuminated initial for a bible.'

The award-winning typo-animation Kapitaal (Capital) shows how today's world contains an overwhelming amount of visual stimuli. By putting it in black and white, Studio Smack questions the commercial effectiveness of this information overload. It makes this animation a fine example of the Design for Debate in which Studio Smack specialises.

1970 | If we weren't so good, why aren't we better
Chermayeff & Geismar
exhibition

2006 | Kapitaal
Studio Smack
typo-animation

Ivan Chermayeff and Tom Geismar, founders of New York-based branding and graphic design firm Chermayeff & Geismar, used their innovative 'supermarket principle' in an exhibition on productivity for the Smithsonian Institution. By grouping all the protective gloves and helmets that American workers could wear, they conveyed a collective idea of safety and the need to improve working conditions.

Three art school students with a preference for small-scale subcultural initiatives, started their design agency 75B in 1997. Eventually their assignments became bigger and more prestigious, like the colour design for the floor of the 6700 m2 skate park on the midsection of the Westblaak, one of Rotterdam's main roads, for CBK (Centrum Beeldende Kunst Rotterdam),

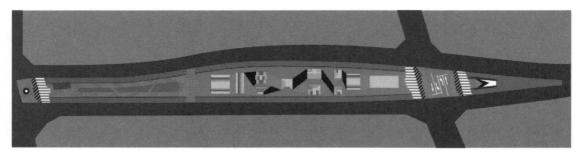

1970 | Nibankan building
Kiyoshi Awazu
mural decoration

2000 | Skate park Westblaak
75B
floor design for CBK

'Back then nobody asked a graphic designer to paint the sides of a building', architect Minoru Takeyama has said about his collaboration with the Japanese graphic designer Kiyoshi Awazu. The acclaimed poster designer devised a 'supergraphic' for the Nibankan building in Tokyo's entertainment district. The idea was to replace the painted design every five years with a new one.

creative commons

American academic and political activist Lawrence Lessig is a fierce advocate of reduced legal restrictions on copyrights. As an alternative, he, together with others, founded the Creative Commons license scheme. Easy to understand pictograms enable people to communicate what others can or cannot do with their creations.

1971 | @
Ray Tomlinson
decision

2001 | Creative Commons
Ryan Junell & Alex Roberts
icons

The @-sign has become an icon for the digital world since American computer programmer Ray Tomlinson back in 1971 chose the sign as the division mark in email addresses. As such it was added by the Museum of Modern Art in New York to its collection. The sign itself stems from the Middle Ages when it was used as a measurement unit for the content of a jug. It developed into a book keeping sign – 10 apples @ 50 cents – and for this reason it figured on the keyboards of computers.

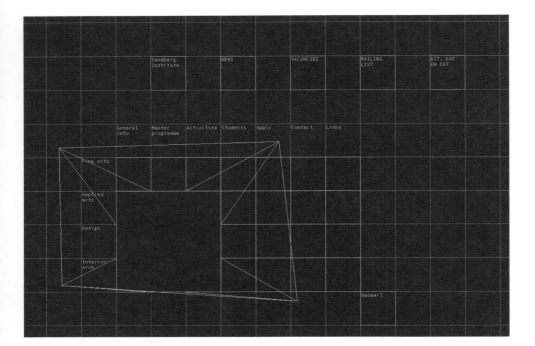

The website for the Amsterdam post graduate design school the Sandberg Institute, has a completely dynamic grid. The size of the grid, the colours, and the positions of the cells can be changed through a content management system. The same goes for the supporting sounds. Developed by Luna Maurer and Edo Paulus, this playful website reflects their philosophy of conditional design.

1971 | Warsaw Autumn 1971
Hubert Hilscher
poster

2007 | Sandberg Instituut
Luna Maurer
website

Technical limitations together with a restrictive political system caused poster art to flourish in Poland between the 1950s and 1980s. The hand drawn posters in vivid colours usually display strong, surprising images, often with hidden messages for those who would understand. Hubert Hilscher was known for his clean compositions with strong hues.

VOLKSWARE
coat
$ 796.987,20

www.volksware.org

If you can't beat it, wear it. In this postmodern classic, preferably worn outside the rain season, designer Silke Wawro has used more than 7,500 brand labels. Well aware of the grotesque power of commercialism, postmodernist designers frequently enter into a complicit relationship with it.

1971 | Van Abbemuseum
Jan van Toorn
poster

2001 | The Most Expensive Coat
Silke Wawro
clothing

VAN ABBEMUSEUM
EINDHOVEN

CHAGALL
DUCHAMP
KANDINSKY
YVES KLEIN
MONDRIAAN
MOHOLY NAGY
PICASSO
f273.969,-+

12 februari tm 28 maart 1971
openingstijden dagelijks 10 tot 5 uur zon- en feestdagen 2 tot 6 uur
dinsdagavond 8 tot 10 uur

Jan van Toorn represents counterculture in the glory days of Dutch modernist graphic design, always opposing Wim Crouwel's militant neutrality. With a strong fascination for materialism and the mechanisms of propaganda, Van Toorn decided to take a stand. In his view designers need not hide themselves behind types or grids.

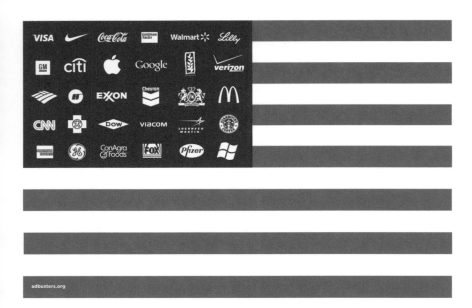

The Corporate America flag is a strong representation of the omnipotent control of corporate America, perfectly fitting in Adbuster's visual battle against the erosion of our physical and cultural environments by commercial forces. The Vancouver-based global network of creative culture jammers use the weapon of pastiche to criticise the dominance of commercial messages.

1976 | Bicentennial Poster U.S.A.
Massimo Vignelli
poster

2000 | Corporate America Flag
Adbusters
flag

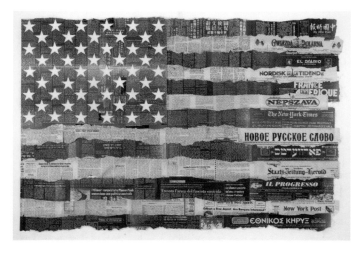

As part of a series for the United States Bicentennial, America's design legend Massimo Vignelli designed a poster to celebrate not a 'melting pot', but the lively interaction of the different ethnic groups in American society. He constructed the American flag out of all the foreign-language newspapers published for different ethnic communities in New York.

This design is one of the few effective and solid adaptations of the über-known I ♥ NY logo, together with Glaser's own adaptation he made in reaction to 9/11 when he changed the logo into saying I ♥ NY More Than Ever. This, however, is a witty representation of today's copy/paste culture that relies strongly on the visual literacy of its viewers.

1977 | I ♥ NY
Milton Glaser
logo

2010 | I Can't Afford to ♥ NY
Clinton van Gemert / Clintees
T-shirt

One of the mythical claims that surround the origins of this logo is that Glaser actually had a tough time convincing his client to use the nonverbal ♥, instead of the word LOVE. This logo is a starting point in the cult of city branding. One might almost overlook the quality of the design, for its omnipresence and frequent appropriation. However Milton Glaser was the first designer to receive the National Medal of Arts, on February 25, 2010.

This videoclip is made with lidar technology which detects the proximity of objects to the sensor. This gives the video a grainy and grid-like appearance. The video was made on a minimal set without any cameras or lights. The data used to make the video was released under Creative Commons Attribution-Noncommercial-Share Alike 3.0 license and is available at Google Code.

1979 | 'Unknown Pleasures' by Joy Division
Peter Saville
album cover

2008 | 'House of Cards' by Radiohead
James Frost & Yon Thomas
music video for XL Recordings

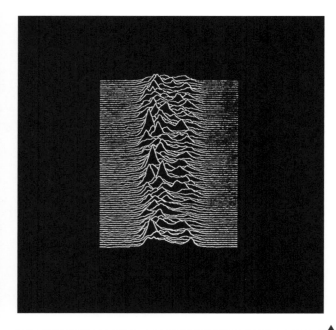

The starting image given by Joy Division to Peter Saville was from an encyclopedia of astronomy. It was a graph recording the radio pulses from a pulsar. Saville commissioned a 3D version of it - an 3D interpretation of this resulted in a sculpture that he calls 'Unknown Pleasures'.

How to mix calligraphic type with scaffolds and get away with it? How to physically transcribe a brand name into the façade of an architectural landmark? Pentagram Studio solved all these problems in one design, when integrating the New York Times logo in a Renzo Piano construction for The New York Times Company and Forest City Ratner Companies.

1980 | Fullscale plotter billboard
Muriel Cooper
technique

2007 | The New York Times Building
Michael Bierut | Pentagram
environmental graphics and signage

Muriel Cooper's legacy has been traced by David Reinfurt in his work 'This Stands as a Sketch for the Future: Muriel Cooper and the Visible Language Workshop'. Cooper was a director of MIT's Visual Language Workshop, here standing in front of a full-scale construction of The Airbrush Plotter. This printer could produce billboard-sized prints from digital files and was designed by Ron MacNeill.

With this perfume, M/M (Paris) reversed the usual idea of receiving a brief from a client. They invited Ben Gorham of Byredo to present him a creative direction and concept - a large utopian formula, a block of solid ink, and a photograph. Resulting in this eau de parfum by Byredo Parfums and M/M (Paris). Art direction and design by M/M (Paris), based on photographs by Inez Van Lamsweerde and Vinoodh Matadin.

Courtesy: mmparis.com

1980 | 'Remain in Light' by Talking Heads
Tibor Kalman
album cover

2010 | M/MINK
M/M (Paris), Van Lamsweerde & Matadin
advertising and promotional posters

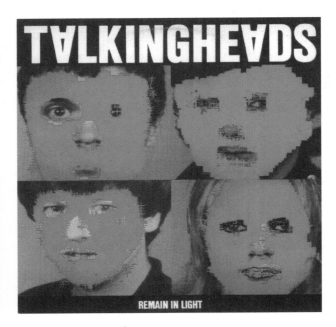

Self-taught graphic designer Tibor Kalman was a committed provocateur. Kalman was inspired by American vernacular design and abundantly mixed loud colours and shapes in his work. He only considered a design successful when it succeeded in bringing messages across that raised social awareness. Kalman contributed to this 1980s album cover of Talking Heads for free, confident in generating attention for his work.

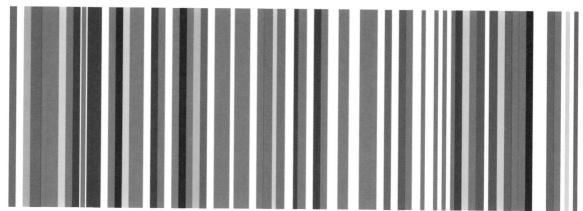

Courtesy: AMO*OMA

Together with AMO, the think tank of his Office for Metropolitan Architecture, architect Rem Koolhaas gave new meaning to the barcode, when he proposed for the client European Comission an additional symbol for the European Union. The EU Barcode merges the flags of current EU member states into a new representative flag, representing Europe as the common effort of different nation states.

1981
Im Mittelpunkt steht immer der Mensch
Klaus Staeck
poster

2006
EU Barcode
Rem Koolhaas, AMO
symbol

Since the introduction of the barcode with twelve digit Universal Product Code in 1973, artists and designers have used the code as a symbol for automation and dehumanisation of society. Take, for example, this poster, Man is always in the centre, by German graphic artist Klaus Staeck, known for his politically conscious and satirical work.

STEREO

LOUIS XIV
THE BEST LITTLE SECRETS ARE KEPT

Louis XIV
FINDING OUT TRUE LOVE
IS BLIND
PAPER DOLL
GOD KILLED THE QUEEN
A LETTER TO Dominique
Illegal TENDER
PLEDGE OF Allegiance
HEY TEACHER
All THE Little Pieces
BAII of TWINE

PARENTAL
ADVISORY
EXPLICIT CONTENT

In without doubt the longest rationale of a design ever, art director John Hofstetter takes 12,000 words to explain the making of the art work for the album The best little secrets are kept by American rock band Louis XIV. The story was quite simple, though: band leader Jason Hill thought it time to stir up prudish America with a nude girl on the cover. Hence the parental advisory sticker.

Photography: Phil Mucci

1981 | Troilus en Cressida
Anton Beeke
poster

2005 | The best little secrets are kept by Louis XIV
Jason Hill, John Hofstetter
album art work

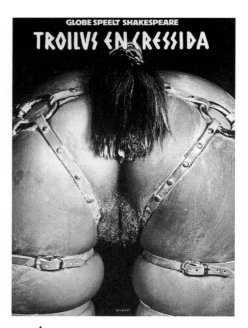

GLOBE SPEELT SHAKESPEARE
TROILVS EN CRESSIDA

Rock, Raw & Roll, was Anton Beeke's device during the late Seventies, while being a key figure in the Dutch New Wave graphic movement. Unafraid and bluntly direct in using sexual codes, Beeke always succeeds in projecting his true dedication and interest for the human body through design.

Design-researchers Daniel van der Velden, Gon Zifroni, and Vinca Kruk together form Metahaven. Through a variety of graphic concepts they aim to create another level of discourse, digesting modern and postmodern influences. Their political messages are stripped bare of the glamorous cliché of design. This poster is called 'Les Européens sont les habitants de L'Europe' and is part of the serie Affiche Frontière.

Courtesy: Metahaven, CAPC musée d'art contemporain de Bordeaux

1982 | Grapus Expo
Grapus
poster

2008 | Affiche Frontière
Metahaven
screen print on paper

Highly engaged design collective Grapus was founded in France after the May '68 student revolt. The poster was their main communicator, out of the desire to be as public as possible. At first glance their highly symbolic messages appear to be explicit and blunt. A closer look reveals a great aesthetic sensibility, inspirational for young graphic designers even today.

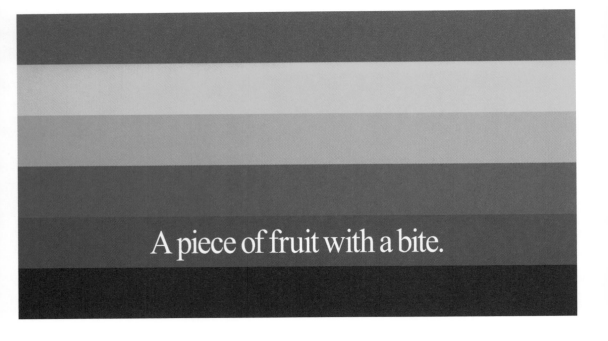

A piece of fruit with a bite.

Beyond Recognition is a performance by Hendrik-Jan Grievink that consists of semantic descriptions of corporate icons, typeset in a recognizable style. When carefully recited as a 'visual poem about corporate identity, brand recognition and the image of words', the maker plays a game of reference with the audience.

1982 | Eye Bee M
Paul Rand
poster for IBM

2006 | Beyond Recognition
Hendrik-Jan Grievink
performance

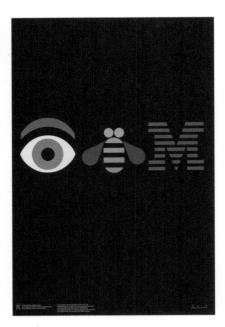

Before anything else, New York-born graphic designer Paul Rand, was a communicator: his multilayered work aims to strengthen the message, rather than comment on it. Rand's images reflect a natural use of basic semiotic principles, elaborated into a childlike poetry. He fervently rejected postmodern theory and aesthetics.

A Cowboy

A Red Star On A Green Bottle.

A Red Planet

The Peace Symbol in Chrome.

A MOUSE WIELDING A MAGIC WAND.

A BLACK COOKIE WITH A WHITE FILLING

A BOTTLE *Creatively Decorated* IN DISGUISE

A Horse Rears On Your Sports Car

A YELLOW FRAME ENCLOSING A TROPICAL FOREST

AN OLD MAN SMILES TO ME

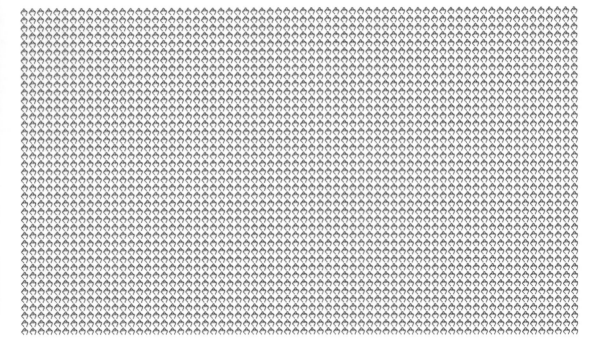

In a nostalgic mood, German-Dutch graphic designer Niels Schrader from Mind Design worked on a poetic visual reference to Apple Macintosh's classic operating system. The work fits into Schrader's conceptual way of designing based on translations of digital information into physical media, and vice versa.

1984 | Icons for Mac
Susan Kare
computer icons

2007 | Homage à Mac OS 9
Niels Schrader | Mind Design
desktop poetry

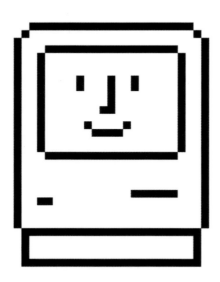

Part of the revolution that Apple Inc. caused in 1984 with the introduction of the Macintosh, was due to the understandable visual metaphors for computer commands which the computer displayed. The icons were developed by graphic designer Susan Kare, who had to confine them within a grid of 30 x 30 pixels. The watch, the bomb, and the trash bin have become classic symbols. And the friendly Mac icon is there to welcome you in.

լշ Հայաստանի արեւանամ բանն եմ ս...
ագի² ողբանուաց, լացականած լարն ե...
ան ծաղիկների ու վարդերի բոյրը վառ...
ան⁴ աղջիկների հեզաճկուն պարն եմ...
մեր երկինքէ մուգ⁵, ջրերը չինչ, լիճր⁶ լ...
ւան ու ձնեռուալ միջապաձայն բուրբ⁷ ...
րած խարճիթների անհիրրընկալ⁸ պատ...
յ քաղաքների հագարանեայ քըն եմ ...

մ չեմ մոնանայ ես ողբացայն երգերր ...
ւայ աղօթք դարձած երկաթագիր գրբե...
նւր սիրտս խոցեն արհինաբքամ վ[ր]ը...
ու արնավատ իմ Հայաստան-եայն եմ ...

ւած սրրտի համար ո՛չ մի ուրիշ հեքիաթ...
ւ¹⁰, Քուչակի¹¹ պես լուսապրսակ¹² ճակա...
ւնցիր¹³, Արարատի նրման ճերմակ զաց...
հնա փաթքի¹⁴ ճամբայ` ես իմ Մասիս ս...

մշակութային

հիմնական ջեռագիր

ինքնակապարեղյագործություն

● Ու նայիրեան աղջիկների
հեզաճկուն պարն եմ սիրում: ●

ճանաչել Ջիմաստություն

արեգ կպապատառ

պզտիկ զինուոր մըն եմ ախբեր

24 Յուլիս 1978

With students from all over the world coming from varied backgrounds, the MA in Type & Media of The Royal Academy in The Hague keeps its respected reputation in the world of type design. A great example of this is the typeface Arek, intended to be used in school books. Arek is a fresh interpretation of the highly elegant Armenian script. By developing this project, type designer Khajag Apelian demonstrates his great potential.

1985 | Hangul alfabet
Ahn Sang-Soo
typeface

2009 | Arek
Khajag Apelian
typeface

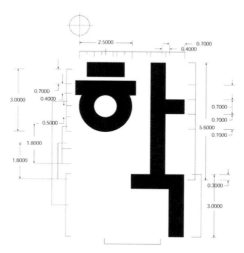

It takes the eye of a poet, the profound mind of a philosopher, and the analytical approach of a graphic designer to embark on an adventure like this. Ahn Sang-Soo, when venturing into the transcription of the ancient Korean language Kangul, turned out to be such an adventurer. The digital realm and the phonologically coded 15th century language proved highly compatible. Sang-Soo's effort was also of an emancipating significance for Korean identity.

Type is speech on paper, Typeradio is speech on type. Pan-European collective of type designers Underware, together with designers Donald Beekman and Liza Enebeis, launched their online radio channel on type and design in 2004. Since then the makers visit design events around the world, to talk to designers about their work.

1986 | Typ/Typografisch Papier Nº 1
Max Kisman
magazine

2004 | Typeradio
Underware, Beekman & Enebeis
internet radio station

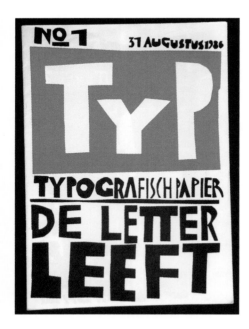

Out of dissatisfaction with all the useless information and bad taste in design and visuals in the early days of the digital age, graphic designer and illustrator Max Kisman initiated Typ/Typographic Paper. The magazine, run with several colleagues, informed about and gave its opinion on image in design, art, and literature. Not its design, but the quality of the content determined the magazine's identity.

'Buy nothing day is your special day to unshop, unspend and unwind.' Thus reads the explanation on www. buynothingday.org. The concept was by Canadian artist Ted Dave and elaborated into a successful campaign by anti-consumerist activist organisation Adbusters.

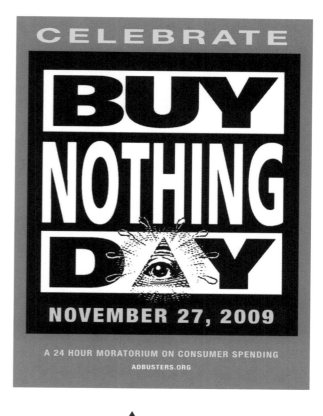

CELEBRATE

BUY NOTHING DAY

NOVEMBER 27, 2009

A 24 HOUR MORATORIUM ON CONSUMER SPENDING

ADBUSTERS.ORG

1987 | Untitled (I shop therefore I am)
Barbara Kruger
photographic silkscreen/vinyl

2007 | Buy Nothing Day
Adbusters
campaign

The simpler the means, the more powerful the message. Photographic close-ups in black-and-white, sans serif type on a red foundation: American collage artist Barbara Kruger can move worlds with only these ingredients. She borrows from history and philosophy, mirrors advertising and propaganda strategies, inverts them, and blasts her message across.

Photography: Marques Malacia

Sport unifies and divides. Well aware of the power of sports symbols, Amsterdam-based designer Floor Wesseling created his Blood in Blood out series around this theme.

1989 | Romanian flag with hole
unknown
flag

2010 | Blood in Blood out
Floor Wesseling
apparel

The importance of flags as national symbols remains. Until 1989 Romania's flag showed a coat of arms. During the struggle in '89, as an act of revolt, people cut out the centre pieces. Their 'holey' flags represent a new era and the courage of the people that fought to bring Ceauçescu's dictatorship to an end.

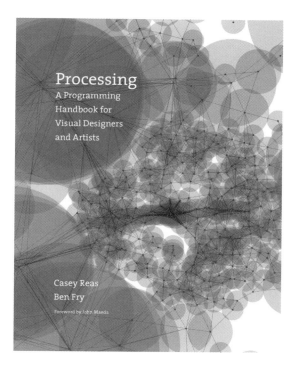

Processing
A Programming
Handbook for
Visual Designers
and Artists

Casey Reas
Ben Fry

Foreword by John Maeda

This amazing open source software serves to create art. Ben Fry and Casey Reas have combined forces in the development of this impressive digital art implement. Processing is in constant development and has already changed radically since 2001. And will continue to do so for the times to come.

1989 | Structures de quadrilatères
Vera Molnar
plotter drawing, ink on paper

2001 | Processing
Casey Reas & Ben Fry
open source software

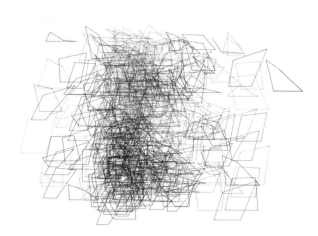

'My work does not contain any elements of a symbolic, metaphysical, or mystical kind, there is no message. Absolutely no message.' Thus states artist Vera Molnar when asked about her work. Molnar was one of the first artists to start integrating computers in her work during the 1960s, for the tool suited her rational approach to geometric form. Frequently Molnar focuses on one shape to build upon the consequences it brings about in space.

Courtesy: Gallery [DAM] Berlin/Cologne I © Harf Zimmermann

Emery Studio provided for a new revolution in directions when they developed the signage for a car park in Melbourne. The distorted letters on the wall and floor can be read perfectly when standing in the right position.

1991 | Signage Schiphol Airport
Paul Mijksenaar
signage

2007 | Eureka Tower car park signage
Emery Studio
signage

Since 1991, Mijksenaar radically updated the revolutionary signage system Benno Wissing designed in 1967 for Schiphol Amsterdam Airport. The colours yellow and green were retained, but Mijksenaar reduced the amount of arrows, added pictograms, and changed the typeface from Akzidenz Grotesk to Frutiger. The signage at Schiphol became a standard for airports around the globe.

MY FEVER
MY SKIN
I CANNOT BREATHE
I CANNOT EAT
I CANNOT WALK
I AM LOSING TIME
I AM LOSING GROUND

'My fever. My skin. I cannot breathe. I cannot eat. I cannot walk. I am losing time. I am losing ground.' (text: Arno, 1996) This is one of the light projections that artist Jenny Holzer makes. Here she projects on the City Hall of Basel, Switzerland.

1991 | Legible city
Jeffrey Shaw
Installation

2009 | For Basel
Jenny Holzer
light Projection

You can literally ride your bike through Alphabet Street in this computer graphic installation by Jeffrey Shaw. New York, Amsterdam, or Karlsruhe, it's up to you where to go. For Shaw created three versions of the interactive game. It appears to be an arty virtual gimmick, the historical layer though has been perfectly worked out. All the letters were scaled, so to represent fully the proportions and locations of the buildings they replace.

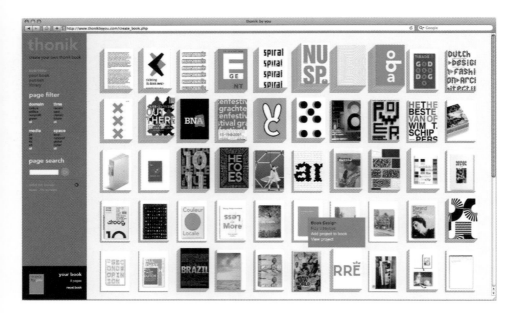

Thonik secretly is a verb. In the Netherlands there is currently no way of getting around the style of the Amsterdam-based design agency. Thonik not only gives a face to many public institutions, the agency now wants you to work with them as a tool. This book is merely the beginning. *Thonik made by you.*

1992 | "Untitled", 1992/1993
Felix González-Torres
print on paper, endless copies

2009 | thonik by you
Thonik
website / print on demand service

Felix González-Torres was a Cuban-born conceptual artist, who became famous in the United States. His work revolved around the tension between the public and the private, originality and authorship. He frequently functioned merely as an assembler, as with these stacks. González-Torres provided the basic pattern within the gallery space, but confidently left it up to the visitor to evolve and give meaning to the work.

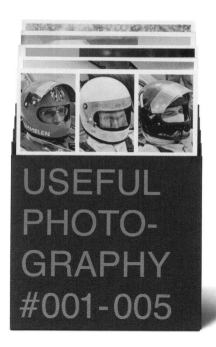

USEFUL
PHOTO-
GRAPHY
#001-005

The Useful Photography series has been collected and edited by Hans Aarsman, Claudie de Cleen, Julian Germain, Erik Kessels and Hans van der Meer. With this series of books, they are recontextualising found photographs and curating them into one collection. As soon as the images are lifted out of their context, they produce new insights into what is considered useful photography.

1993	Getty Images, Inc. Mark Getty and Jonathan Klein company	**2008**	Useful Photography Kesselskramer Publishing book

gettyimages®

In 1993, Mark Getty and Chief Executive Officer Jonathan Klein co-founded Getty Investments LLC. Mark Getty is the company's chairman. Getty Images, Inc. is a stock photo agency. It is a supplier of stock images for business and consumers with an archive of 80 million still images and illustrations and more than 50,000 hours of stock film footage.

  gettyimages®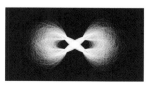

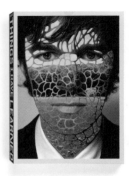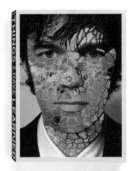
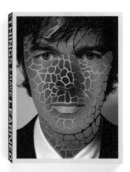

Austrian-born designer Stefan Sagmeister likes to keep score of things, and many of his designs therefore include listings. Predominantly his designs are self centred and pretty bold. As master Sagmeister points out himself: Having guts always works out. (thing number 20)

Cover portrait photography: Henry Leutwyler

1994 | Kunst Rai
Anthon Beeke
poster

2008 | Things I have learned so far in my life
Stefan Sagmeister & Matthias Ernstberger
book

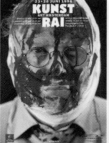

Between 1994 and 2002, Anton Beeke designed posters for the Amsterdam Kunst Rai. Beeke applied his provocative skills, remaining true to one concept. Every year he portrayed the most acclaimed character of that time in the Dutch art world, covering him with a mask. Rudi Fuchs, Jeroen Henneman, and Benno Premsela were subsequently on Beeke's list, drenched in blood, laced in rope, or painted. Their disguise made reference to an edgy happening of that year.

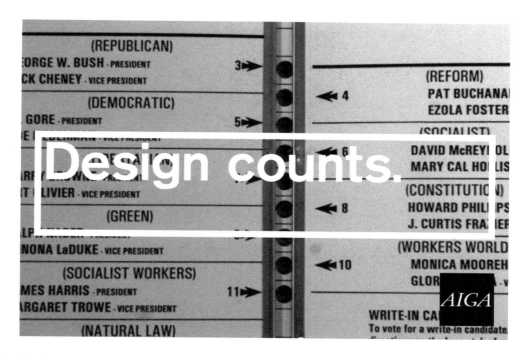

Design counts.

AIGA

Michael Bierut is a leading and inspirational figure in the world of design. He is a designer with a cause. This cause is not so much an object or aspect that has to be achieved through design; it is the intrinsic value of it. Bierut defends the standards of design with a critical eye, in a way comparable to environmental activism. Voting ballots, though, are Bierut's puppy seals.

1997 | Excerpt from 'Visual Explanations'
Edward R. Tufte
information visualization

2001 | Design Counts
Michael Bierut | Pentagram
poster for AIGA

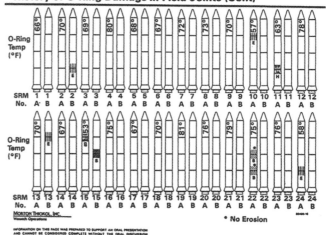

This image is the 'Report of the Presidential Commission on the Space Shuttle Challenger Accident' (Washington DC, 1986). Edward R. Tufte takes this as an example in his book 'Visual Explanations' (Graphics Press, 1997) to eloquently state the importance of well-designed information visualizations.

Feeling All   Gender Both   Age All   Weather All   Location All   Date All

i feel so alone and this is just another time when i want to go hide where no one will ever find me

7 hours ago / from someone in henderson north carolina united states

Madness
Murmurs
Montage
Mobs
Metrics
Mounds

Jonathan Harris is the virtual harvester of hearts. This artist designs online projects that aim to sensitise the virtual reality we ourselves create. In an attempt to map our collective emotional landscape, the search engine website 'We Feel Fine' roams the interwebs for feelings. Daily, thousands of new ones are carefully bundled into its database. They provide an emotive diagnosis of the world.

1999 | SequoiaView
TU/e Visualization group (J.J. Wijk)
software

2009 | We feel fine
Jonathan Harris & Sep Kamvar
website

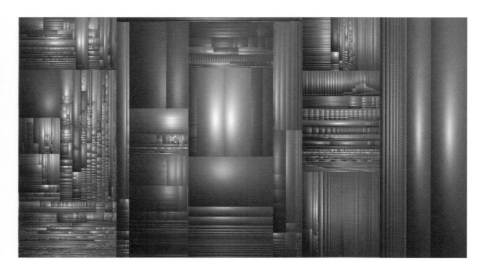

SequoiaView visualizes information using shaded cushions on top of a treemap, to create visual insights in large hierarchical data sets, such as directory structures and organization structures. This particular image shows Van Wijk's own hard drive content.

American artist Barbara Kruger cites Orwell's 1984 in her dystopic installation. The meaning of the word seems to be abstracted from the message, since the letters have been blown out of proportion. Typefaces spill over from floor to walls and ominously hang over the spectator.

1999 | The Child / Alex Gopher
H5
video clip

2010 | Human
Barbara Kruger
installation

New York City, night time, crazy traffic. Will the taxi get the pregnant lady to the hospital on time? Billie Holliday sings the tune to this track by French dj Alex Gopher. The video was made by H5. They spice up the story by transcribing the entire city and its protagonists into type. Through a minimum of information H5 create a mysterious atmosphere, just as strong as good old cinema.

INDEX

GRAPHIC DESIGN 1900 - 2000

page 52

1　　2　　3　　4　　5　　6　　7　　8

page 53

1　　**2**　　3　　4　　5　　6　　7

page 54

1　　2　　**3**　　4　　5　　6　　7

page 55

1　　2　　**3**　　4　　5　　6

page 56

1　　2　　3　　4　　5　　**6**　　7

PAGE 52
1. Ver Sacrum, Koloman Moser, 1899
2. Ubu, Alfred Jarry, 1899
3. Big Gaiety Spectacular Extravaganza, The Courier Company 1900
4. Wiener Werkstaette, Josef Hoffmann & Koloman Moser, 1903
5. A stenciled calendar for 1904, Edward Penfield, 1904
6. Priester, Lucian Bernhard, 1905
7. Theo Heemskerk, Albert Hahn Sr, 1911
8. Nerven-Ruhe Kaffee Hag, Eduard Scotland & Alfred Runge, 1912

PAGE 53
1. Stemt Rood! (Vote Red!), Albert Hahn, 1913
2. Michelin, Marius Rossillon, 1913
3. Journal 291, Marius de Zayas, 1915
4. Beat Germany, Adolph Treidler, 1917
5. I Want You For US Army, James Montgomery Flagg, 1917
6. Hey Fellows!, John E. Sheridan, 1918
7. USS Leviathan In 'Dazzle Camouflage', Norman Wilkinson, 1918

PAGE 54
1. Beat the Whites, El Lissitzky, 1919
2. In The Evening, Lying on her bed, she reread the letter from her artilleryman at the front, Filippo Marinetti, 1919

3. Monogram for JJP Oud, Theo van Doesburg, 1919
4. Dadaphone, Francis Picabia, 1920
5. La Section d'Or, Theo van Doesburg, 1920
6. Gorod. Stikhi (The City. Verse), Alexander Roubakine, 1920
7. Linocut, László Moholy-Nagy, 1920

PAGE 55
1. Bezette stad (Occupied City), Oskar Jespers, 1921
2. Notgeld (Emergency Money), Wenzel Hablik, 1921
3. Boem Paukeslag, Paul Van Ostaijen, 1921
4. Dada stirs up everything, Filippo Marinetti, 1921
5. Wendingen, El Lissitzky, 1921
6. Vermögensabgabe NEIN (No Tax on Fortune), Emil Cardinaux, 1922

PAGE 56
1. Diagram of Bauhaus Curriculum, Johannes Itten, 1922
2. A4, based on the German DIN 476 standard, 1922
3. Bauhaus logo, Oskar Schlemmer, 1922
4. BP Motor Spirit, unknown, 1922
5. Broom Vol.4, El Lissitzky, 1922
6. V Invest, unknown, 1922
7. Winter sales are best reached by underground, Edward McKnight Kauffer, 1922

page 57

  ...

   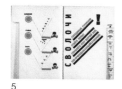

1   2   3   4   5   6   7

page 58

   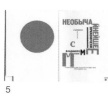

1   2   3   4   5   6   7

page 60

1   2   3   4   5   6   7

page 61

1   2   3   4   5   6

page 62

1   2   3   4   5   6   7   8

PAGE 57
1. Le Cœur à barbe (The Bearded Heart), Hans Arp, 1922
2. Time magazine cover 1st issue, unknown, 1923
3. Broom Vol.5, El Lissitzky, 1923
4. Wat is Dada?, Theo van Doesburg, 1923
5. For the voice, El Lissitzky, 1923
6. Shestaya chast mira, Aleksandr Rodchenko, 1923
7. Ad for Mosselprom Oil, Aleksandr Rodchenko & Vladimir Mayakovsky, 1923

PAGE 58
1. Red October Biscuit, Aleksandr Rodchenko, 1923
2. ABCD, Raoul Hausman, 1923
3. Bauhaus, Joost Schmidt, 1923
4. Ad for Baby-Food Nipples, Aleksandr Rodchenko, 1923
5. Dlya Golosa (For The Voice), El Lissitzky, 1923
6. Metropolis, Paul Citroen, 1923
7. The Print is our Weapon, Varvara Stepanova & Aleksandr Rodchenko, 1923

PAGE 60
1. Design for sports clothing, Varvara Stepanova, 1923
2. Verwende stets nur Gas (Always use only gas for cooking), Walter Dexel, 1924
3. Brightest London, Horace Taylor, 1924
4. Dicke Bohnen, Valentin Zietara, 1924

5. N.E.T.H.M.IJ, Piet Zwart, 1924
6. Laugh Clown Laugh, Batiste Madalena, 1924
7. Theatre magazine, Charles Baskerville, 1924

PAGE 61
1. Kino Glaz, Aleksandr Rodchenko, 1924
2. Design for a newspaper kiosk, Herbert Bayer, 1924
3. Merz, El Lissitzky, 1924
4. Ad on Wall of Mosselprom building, Aleksandr Rodchenko, 1924
5. Kukirol, Stenberg Brothers, 1925
6. Sturm Blond, Herbert Bayer, 1925

PAGE 62
1. Exhibition poster, Murayama Tomoyoshi, 1925
2. Herkules Bier, Ludwig Hohlwein, 1925
3. Olly & Dolly Sisters, László Moholy-Nagy , 1925
4. De Unie, JJP Oud, 1925
5. Aesthete, Charles Sheeler, 1925
6. The Little Review Gallery, Theo van Doesburg, 1925
7. Superior Dutch Ham Berkel, Paul Schuitema, 1925
8. Photogram, László Moholy-Nagy, 1926

page 63

1

2

3

4

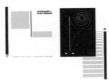
5

page 64

1

2

3

4

5

6

7

8

page 65

1

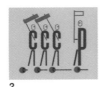
2

3

4

5

6

7

page 66

1

2

3

4

5

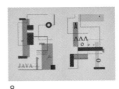
6

page 67

1

2

3

4

5

6

7

PAGE 63
1. Mitropa, Gerd Arntz, 1925
2. A Alphabet, Karel Teige, 1926
3. Vierkant en Plat Draad, Piet Zwart, 1926
4. Vierkant Plat Rond, Piet Zwart, 1926
5. 1st logo HEMA, unknown, 1929

PAGE 64
1. Upward, Josef Albers, 1926
2. De Ploeg, H.N. Werkman, 1927
3. Die Frau ohne Namen, Jan Tschichold, 1927
4. The Enemy, Wyndham Lewis, 1927
5. Kalender, H.N. Werkman, 1927
6. London Magazine, Tom Purvis, 1927
7. Novyi Lef, Aleksandr Rodchenko, 1927
8. Java, Karel Teige, 1928

PAGE 65
1. Nutricia, Paul Schuitema, 1927
2. Josephine Baker in Papitoe, Dolly Rudeman, 1927
3. Philips Radio, Louis Kalff, 1927
4. Wordt wakker!, Albert Hahn jr, 1927
5. The Pretender, Stenberg Brothers, 1927
6. Metropolis, Boris Bilinsky, 1927
7. From 21 February Leningradodezhda lowered prices on their goods, Dmitry Anatol'evich Bulanov, 1927

PAGE 66
1. Book Pavillion, Fortunato Depero, 1927
2. Depero Futurista, Fortunato Depero, 1927
3. Life, Coles Philips, 1927
4. Nederlandsche Kabelfabriek, Piet Zwart, 1927
5. Kabelfabriek, Piet Zwart, 1928
6. Champion sparkplugs ad, Lanfranco Felin, 1928

PAGE 67
1. Swiss advertisement for voting regarding Kursaals legislation, unknown, 1928
2. Die Vier Grundrechnungsarten, El Lissitzy, 1928
3. WRNY Radio Advertisement, Experimenter Publishing, 1928
4. Advertisement for Swiss voting of 1929 against spirits, Jules Courvoisier, 1929
5. Kult und Form, Walter Dexel, 1929
6. Rubbol, unknown, 1929
7. A Man of Fire, Nikolay Petrovich Prusakov, 1929

page 68

1

2

3

4

5

6

7

page 69

1

2

3

4

5

6

7

8

page 70

1

2

3

4

5

6

7

8

page 72

1

2

3

4

5

6

7

page 73

1

2

3

4

5

6

7

PAGE 68
1. AvantGarde, Vasyl Yermylov, 1929
2. Man with the Movie Camera, Stenberg Brothers, 1929
3. Potemkin, Stenberg Brothers, 1929
4. Ad for French car Rochet-Schneider, unknown, 1930
5. Der Rote 1 Mark Roman, Alex Keil, 1930
6. Lampo, Marcello Nizzoli, 1930
7. New York, Fortunato Depero, 1930

PAGE 69
1. Centrale Bond, Paul Schuitema, 1930
2. Football World Cup Uruguay, unknown, 1930
3. Gran Bazar, Lucio Venna, 1930
4. Isotype / At Work, Gerd Arntz, 1930
5. Kabels voor Kas-verwarming, Piet Zwart, 1930
6. Modiano, Federico Seneca, 1930
7. Montage Selbstportrait, Hajo Rose, 1930
8. Clovek nikdy neví (You never can tell), Ladislav Sutnar, 1931

PAGE 70
1. Amerikaansche Filmkunst, Piet Zwart, 1931
2. Catalogue Page, Piet Zwart, 1931
3. Koopt ten bate van het misdeelde kind, Gerard Kiljan, 1931
4. Transforming Moscow into a model socialist city, Aleksandr Dejneka, 1931
5. Vanity Fair, Jean Carlu, 1931

6. **Zuid-Holland Rood!, Meijer Bleekrode, 1931**
7. Quality League Settlement, Joseph Binder, 1932
8. Vogue (1st color photo cover), Mehemed Fehmy Agha & Edward Steichen, 1932

PAGE 72
1. Typografische Entwurfstechnik, Jan Tschichold, 1932
2. Ik wacht 5 min, N.P. De Koo, 1933
3. LISTROY, Vasyl Yermylov, 1933
4. London Underground, Harry Beck, 1933
5. National Recovery Act, Charles Coiner, 1933
6. Van Nelle gebroken thee, Jac. Jongert, 1933
7. Wer rechnet kauft im Globus, Otto Baumberger, 1934

PAGE 73
1. Paimio Chair, Alvar Aalto, 1933
2. Campari Pavillion, Fortunato Depero, 1933
3. Buitoni Pasta Ad, Federico Seneca, 1934
4. Ulysses, Ernst Reichl, 1934
5. Der Deutsche Student, Ludwig Hohlwein, 1936
6. Don't Mix 'em, Robert Lachenmann, 1937
7. PM, Lester Beall, 1937

page 74

1   2   3   4   5   **6**   7

page 75

      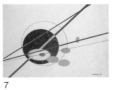

1   2   3   4   5   6   7   8

page 76

1   2   **3**   4   5   6   7   8

page 77

1   2   3   4   5   6   7

page 78

1   2   3   4   5   6   7

PAGE 74
1. Keep Calm and Carry On, unknown, 1939
2. Smash Song Hits, Alex Steinweiss, 1939
3. America Calling, Herbert Matter, 1940
4. Direction, Paul Rand, 1940
5. Freedom Shall Prevail, unknown, 1940
6. The Men Are Ready, unknown, 1940
7. Twenty-Third Commencement, Alvin Lustig, 1940

PAGE 75
1. Pitto is best, Pieter Den Besten, 1940
2. Baumann, Otto Baumberger, 1940
3. Beware of the Swarf, Leonard Cusden, 1940
4. Buy British, Tom Purvis, 1940
5. Can Al You Can, unknown, 1940
6. Chocolat Amor, Merz, 1940
7. Composizione n.16, Luigi Veronesi, 1940
8. Douglas Aircraft Company Ad, unknown, 1940

PAGE 75
1. Get Skilled Aid, Manfred Reiss, 1940
2. Inspect Daily, Tom Eckersley, 1940
3. Clean packages instead of dirty hands, Herbert Matter, 1940
4. La Battaglia del Grano, RAM (Ruggero Alfredo Michahelles), 1940

5. Linee Italiane per tutto il Mondo, unknown, 1940
6. Lucky Strikes Redesign, Rymond Loewy, 1940
7. Neuheit - Indiana, unknown, 1940
8. Philips, Cavadini, 1940

PAGE 77
1. The world according to standard (N.J.), Richard Edes Harrison, 1940
2. AD magazine, Alex Steinweiss, 1941
3. Air Corps US Army, Joseph Binder, 1941
4. A Woman's Face, unknown, 1941
5. Keep your Mouth Shut, Vatolina & Denisov, 1941
6. Me Worry?, Norman Mingo, 1941
7. Report Dog Bites, Earl Schuler, 1941

PAGE 78
1. Labor, Joseph Binder, 1941
2. Gift packages for Hitler!, Jean Carlu, 1942
3. We Can Do It, J. Howard Miller, 1942
4. Ovenall toothpaste Ad, Zoltan Tamasi, 1942
5. Production, Jean Carlu, 1942
6. I've found the job, George Roepp, 1943
7. UN, Oliver Lincoln Lundquist, 1945

1   2   **3**   4   5   6   7   8

1   2   **3**   4   5   6   7   8

1   2   3   4   5   6   7

1   2   3   **4**   5   6   7

       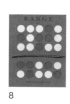

1   2   3   4   5   6   7   8

PAGE 79
1. Weerbare Democratie, Dick Elffers, 1946
2. Atomic Clock, Martyl, 1947
3. Herstel Gehavend Nederland door Arbeid, Wim Brusse, 1947
4. Nationale Reclasseeringsdag, Eppo Doeve, 1947
5. The Great Gatsby, Jan Tschichold, 1947
6. Autodrome Nazionale di Monza, Max Huber, 1948
7. De Schaduw Grijpt In, Bob Mohr, 1948
8. Alhambra Het Huis der Dapperen, Ad Werner, 1949

PAGE 80
1. Autonomous living unit, R. Buckminster Fuller, 1949
2. Borsalino, Max Huber, 1949
3. Picasso Uses Light-Pen, Pablo Picasso & Gjon Milli, 1949
4. Für das Alter, Carlo Vivarelli, 1949
5. LIFE, unknown, 1949
6. Polska, Henryk Tomaszewski, 1949
7. Seventeen, Cipe Pineles, 1949
8. The gay bandit of the border, unknown, 1949

PAGE 82
1. Joy, Cornelius van Velzen, 1949
2. I have nothing to say, Alan Fletcher, 1950
3. Tigra, Al Moore, 1950
4. Typeface Specimen, Elaine Lustig Cohen, 1950

5. Fortune 500, Walter Allner, 1951
6. Wire Mesh Chair, Charles & Ray Eames, 1951
7. I like Ike, unknown, 1952

PAGE 83
1. Association ofAmerican Railroads, Joseph Binder, 1952
2. Lonique, Victor Vasarely, 1952
3. Notre Temps, Frans Masereel, 1952
4. Schützt das Kind, Josef Müller-Brockmann, 1952
5. Esquire, Henry Wolf, 1953
6. I will try, Alvin Lustig, 1953
7. Logo BBC, Abram Games, 1953

PAGE 84
1. De Appel, Dick Bruna, 1953
2. Playboy logo, Art Paul, 1953
3. New Haven Railroad, Herbert Matter, 1954
4. Olivetti Studio 44, Giovanni Pintori, 1954
5. Raffia, Henk Krijger, 1954
6. Herman Miller Furniture Ad, George Tscherny, 1955
7. Man with Golden Arm, Saul Bass, 1955
8. Range, Alexander Raateland & Ton Verberne, 1955

1   2   3   4   5   6   7   8

    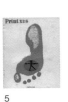   

1   2   3   4   5   6   7   8

1   2   3   4   5   6   7   8

1   2   3   4   5   6   7

1   2   3   4   5   6   7   8

PAGE 85
1. Smalfilmskolan, Rolf Lagerson, 1955
2. Beethoven, Josef Müller-Brockmann, 1955
3. Air France, Raymond Savignac, 1956
4. Anatomy of Revolution, Paul Rand, 1956
5. Experimenta Typografica 11, Willem Sandberg, 1956
6. NBC, John J. Graham, 1956
7. Picasso Exhibition, George Tscherny, 1957
8. Gebrauchsgraphik Magazine, unknown, 1965

PAGE 86
1. Pirelli, scooter, Max Huber, 1957
2. Citroen Ami6 MEER, Karel Suyling, 1958 - 1971
3. Citroen Ami6 WAAROM ZO, Karel Suyling, 1958 - 1971
4. Fanfare, Jan van Keulen, 1958
5. Print XI:6, Saul Bass, 1958
6. Rietveld CMU, Gerrit Rietveld, 1958
7. The Philosophy of Spinoza, Elaine Lustig Cohen, 1958
8. West Virginia Pulp and Paper, Bradbury Thompson, 1958

PAGE 88
1. Die Gute Form, Emil Ruder, 1958
2. British Nuclear Disarmament Movement, Gerald Holtom, 1958
3. Olivetti Graphika, Giovanni Pintori, 1959
4. Olma, Josef Müller-Brockmann, 1959

5. PLEM, Cas Oorthuys, 1959
6. Graphic Design 1st Issue, Tanaka Ikko, 1959
7. Pickpocket, Hans Hillman, 1959
8. Provocative percussion, Josef Albers, 1959

PAGE 89
1. Pirelli + km, Alan Fletcher, 1959
2. A Moral Philosophy for Management, Rudolph De Harak, 1959
3. Collage for Walt Disney Magazine, unknown, 1959
4. Cool Man Cool, Arnold Varga, 1959
5. Watching Words Move, Tom Geismar & Ivan Chermayeff, 1959
6. Czarna Carmen, Wojciech Fangor, 1959
7. Dangling Man, Elaine Lustig, 1959

PAGE 90
1. Duke Ellington, Erwin Meierhofer, 1959
2. Kennedy for President, unknown, 1959
3. Moody Woody, Alex Steinweiss, 1959
4. PingPong, Roy Kuhlman, 1959
5. Pirelli per lo Scooter, Lora Lamm, 1959
6. Pirelli rolle, Bob Noorda, 1959
7. The amazing Nina Simone, unknown, 1959
8. Volkswagen Think Small, Doyle Dane Bernbach, 1959

page 91

1 2 3 4 5 6 7 8

page 92

1 2 3 4 5 6 7 8

page 93

1 2 3 4 5 6 7 8

page 94

1 2 3 4 5 6

page 96

1 2 3 4 5 6 7 8

PAGE 91
1. 1984 by George Orwell, Olle Eksell, 1959
2. Anatomy of Murder, Saul Bass, 1959
3. Cards of Identity, Rudolph De Harak, 1960
4. Books Add a Lot, Louis Silverstein, 1960
5. Dans van de Reiger, Nicolaas Wijnberg, 1960
6. Design cover, Ken Garland, 1960
7. General Dynamics, Erik Nitsche, 1960
8. Luigi Franchi, Aldo Calabresi, 1960

PAGE 92
1. Helgon & Het sporrar, Olle Eksell, 1960
2. Howard Wise Gallery, Chermayeff & Geismar, 1960
3. The Chairs by Ionesco, John Melin & Anders Österlin, 1960
4. The Misfits, Don Ervin & George Nelson, 1960
5. Al-ahmad behrengi deKhoda hedayat, Guity Novin, 1961
6. Idea 45, Hirochi Ohchi, 1961
7. Rock 'n Roll Bata, Herbert Leupin, 1961
8. Taptoe Delft, Otto Treumann, 1961

PAGE 93
1. Catch-22, Paul Bacon, 1961
2. illustration, Robert Miles Runyan, 1961
3. Judy Garland, unknown, 1961
4. Letztes Jahr in Marienbad, Hans Hillman, 1961
5. Moving, Ralph Casado, 1961

6. New Maps of Hell, Milton Glaser, 1961
7. The Future of Man, William R. Gregory, 1961
8. The Rising Gorge, Ben Shahn, 1961

PAGE 94
1. Mieszkanie Nr 8, Roman Cieslewicz, 1961
2. Pirelli, André Francois, 1961
3. Provocative Percussion, Charles Murphy, 1961
4. spread Rover, René Bittle, 1961
5. Vivaldi Gloria, Rudolph De Harak, 1961
6. Advertising Graphics, H. William Bockus Jr, 1969

PAGE 96
1. Amerika by Franz Kafka, Gilda Kuhlman, 1961
2. Modern Publicity, unknown, 1961
3. Show #1, Henry Wolf, 1961
4. SOS Titanic, Wojciech Zamecznik, 1961
5. Too Bad She's Bad, unknown, 1961
**6. You don't have to be Jewish to love Levys, William Taubin-
   Howard Zieff, 1961**
7. Prawo Gwaltu, Maciej Zbikowski, 1973
8. Visual design in Action, Ladislav Sutnar, 1961

page 97

1 2 3 4 5 6 7 8

page 98

1 2 **3** 4 5 6 7

page 99

1 **2** 3 4 5 6 7

page 100

1 2 **3** 4 5 6 7

page 102

1 **2** 3 4 5 6 7 8

PAGE 97

1. Typographische Monatsblätter, Emil Ruder, 1961
2. The Birds, Bronislaw Zenek, 1963
3. Telecommunication, Otto Treumann, 1962
4. Obsession and Fantasy, Robert Brownjohn, 1963
5. Pagina Magazine Nr 2, Bob Noorda, 1963
6. Steppenwolf, unknown, 1963
7. Stop Nuclear Suicide, FHK Henrion, 1963
8. Sein oder Nicht Sein, Hans Hillman, 1964

PAGE 98
1. Dr Strangelove, Pablo Ferro, 1964
2. Enoch Light, Charles Murphy, 1964
3. First Things First, Ken Garland, 1964
4. India Ink, Seymour Chwast, 1964
5. Mission in Guemo, unknown, 1964
6. Modern Houses, Arthur Lockwood, 1964
7. The Sound Album, Sam Suliman, 1964

PAGE 99
1. Men at Work, Margaret Calvert & Jock Kinneir, 1964
2. International Wool Secretariat symbol, Francesco Saroglia, 1964
3. cover for H. Stazewski, J. Stanny, 1965
4. Plastics Today 23, Fletcher Forbes Gill, 1965
5. Telefunken, Jacques Nathan Garamond, 1965

6. Third Mind, William Burroughs & Brion Gysin, 1965
7. Unity, Reid Miles, 1965 1966

PAGE 100
1. Ashai Beer, Kazumasa Nagai, 1965
2. I was Dead, Tadanori Yokoo, 1965
3. AH logo, James Pilditch, 1965
4. PAM auto, Total Design, 1965
5. PAM logo, Total Design, 1965
6. This Must Be the Place, Roy Lichtenstein, 1965
7. Voorjaarsbeurs Utrecht, Otto Treumann, 1965

PAGE 102
1. Death in paradise, Masao Ikeda, 1965
2. Olivetti, Enzo Mari, 1956
3. Ambit 29, Martin Foreman, 1966
4. Die Einsamkeit des Langstreckenlaufers, Hans Hillman, 1966
5. Ma Bells Restaurant, George Lois, 1966
6. Panzerkreuzer Potemkin, Hans Hillmann, 1966
7. Stage Fright, Marek Freudenreich, 1966
8. The Association Along Comes Mary Quicksilver Messenger Service, Wes Wilson, 1966

page 103

1 2 3 4 5 6 7 8

page 104

1 2 3 4 5 6 7 8

page 105

1 2 3 **4** 5 6 7 8

page 106

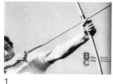

1 2 3 4 **5** 6 7

page 107

1 2 **3** 4 5 6 7 8

PAGE 103
1. Screentests, Andy warhol, 1963 - 1966
2. Kompas 3, Jan van Toorn, 1967
3. Chambers Brothers, Victor Moscoso, 1967
4. Mona Lisa, Roman Cieslewicz, 1967
5. Plant A Flower Child, Martin Sharp & Bob Whitaker, 1967
6. Schiphol Signage, Benno Wissing | Total Design, 1967
7. Studio Hoera Amerika, Jan Bons, 1967
8. Yardbirds, Bonnie MacLean, 1967

PAGE 104
1. New Alphabet, Wim Crouwel, 1966
2. Monterey International Pop Festival, Tom Wilkes, 1967
3. Oedipus At Hiroshima, Mitsuhiro Kushida, 1967
4. REV-UP for IBM, Johannes Reyn, 1967
5. The Little Match Girl, Kushida Mitsuhiro, 1967
6. Typographie, Emil Ruder, 1967
7. Using the pen as a weapon to denounce (Counter-Revolutionary) Black Culture, Dong Jiansheng, 1967
8. New York Shakespeare Festival, Paul Davis, 1967

PAGE 105
1. ?, Martti Mykkanen, 1967
2. Assymmetric Typography, Jan Tschichold, 1967
3. Sgt. Pepper's Lonely Hearts Club Band, Robert Fraser, 1967
4. Bob Dylan, Milton Glaser, 1967

5. Cool Hand Luke, unknown, 1967
6. EAT, Tomi Ungerer, 1967
7. Esquires LBJ cover, Richard Hess Samuel Antupit, 1967
8. Love Festival, Michael English, 1967

PAGE 106
1. Chemical Industry, Atelier Eidenbenz, 1967
2. Doktor Freud, Maciej Zbokowski, 1967
3. Geigy, Fred Troller, 1967
4. L'Influx nerveux de la contraction musculaire, Pascalini, 1967
5. New Darmstadt Secession exhibition poster, Helmut Lortz, 1967
6. OZ, Martin Sharp, 1967
7. River of No Return, Kazimierz Lrolikowski, 1967

PAGE 107
1. Collection of Stories, Tadanori Yokoo, 1967
2. No More War, Kelichi Tanaami, 1967
3. The Velvet Underground, Andy Warhol, 1967
4. 101st Airborne Division shoulder sleeve insignia (the 'Screaming Eagle'), 1968
5. Cover of Lincoln Center Journal, Cipe Pineles, 1968
6. Das Druckgrafische Werk, Max Bill, 1968
7. NS Logo, Tel Design, 1968
8. Vacant World by The Jacks, Takt Label, 1968

1   2   3   4   5   6   7

1   2   3   4   5   6

1   2   3   4   5   6   7   8   9

1   2   3   4   5   6   7

1   2   3   4   5   6   7

PAGE 108
1. End Bad Breath, Seymour Chwast, 1968
2. Blowing In The Mind, Martin Sharp, 1968
3. Joujouka, William Burroughs & Brion Gysin, 1968
4. Rolling Stone, Heinz Edelmann, 1968
5. Sitoon, Guy Debord, 1968
6. T-Shirt Design, Yoshitaro Isaka, 1968
7. The New York Free Press, Steven Heller, 1968

PAGE 109
1. Illinois Sesquicentennial, LeRoy Winbush, 1968
2. Mexico 68, L.Wyman P.Ramirez-Vazquez E.Terrezas, 1968
3. Huisstijl Ahoy, Benno Wissing, 1969
4. Jimi Hendrix Experience, Günther Kieser, 1969
5. Kokusai International Travel, Jim Miho, 1969
6. Marilyn Monroe, Tadanori Yokoo, 1969

PAGE 110
1. Julius Caesar, Dan Reisinger, 1964
2. 2y, Jack W. Stauffacher, 1969
3. 3 Days Of Peace & Music, Arnold Skolnick, 1969
4. BAUHAUS, Muriel Cooper, 1969
5. COBOL, Dietmar Winkler, 1969
6. Najemny Morderca, Jersy Flisak, 1969
7. Reflections In A Mirage And The Ticking Is In Your Head,
   Emanuel Schongut, 1969

8. Welcome 69, unknown, 1969
9. Black & White Scotch Whiskey, AG&M, 1969

PAGE 111
1. Chupa Chups, Salvador Dali, 1969
2. Funeral Parade Roses, Setsu Asakura, 1969
3. Let It Bleed by Rolling Stones, Robert Brownjohn & Don
   McAllester, 1969
4. Rules For Radicals, unknown, 1969
5. Sinalco, Peter Emch, 1969
6. Sweet Corn Herman Miller Picnic Poster, Steve Frykholm 1970
7. Heroina, Andrej Krajewski, 1969

PAGE 112
1. Fernando Arrabal, Roman Cieslewicz, 1970
2. Psycho, Zdenek Ziegler, 1970
3. radioNL, Sam Beek, 1970
4. Recycle, Gary Anderson, 1970
5. The Naked Ladies alphabet, Anthon Beeke, 1971
6. Besos Robados, Rene, 1970
7. Q And babies? A And babies, Art Workers Coalition, 1970

1

2

3

4

5

6

7

1

2

3

4

5

6

7

1

2

3

4

5

6

7

1

2

3

4

5

6

7

8

1

2

3

4

5

6

7

PAGE 113
1. Amerika Is Devouring Its Children, Jay Belloli, 1970
2. Idea Magazine Japan, Alex Steinweiss, 1970
3. If we weren't so good, why aren't we better, Chermayeff & Geismar, poster, 1970
4. If we weren't so good, why aren't we better, Chermayeff & Geismar, exhibition, 1970
5. Santana, unknown, 1970
6. The MOD Squad, unknown, 1970
7. The Other, unknown, 1970
8. Traffic, unknown, 1970

PAGE 114
1. Nibankan, Kiyoshi Awazu, 1970
2. Anti-War, Kiyoshi Awazu, 1971
3. Acoustic Research Contemporary Music Project, Dietmar Winkler, 1971
4. Electronic Revolution, Brion Gysin, 1971
5. European Journal of Social, Juriaan Schrofer, 1971
6. Goya, Jacqueline Casey, 1971
7. Wonderland, Tadanori Yokoo, 1971

PAGE 115
1. Ashes To Ashes, Lawrence Ratzkin, 1971
2. Badz WPorcie Noca, Jerzy Treutler, 1971
3. Book cover for Penguin Education series, Derek Birdsall, 1971

4. @, Ray Tomlinson, 1971
5. Equus, Gilbert Lesser, 1971
6. Libertad Para Angela Davis, Felix Beltran, 1971
7. Tongue And Lip Design, John Pasche, 1971

PAGE 116
1. A Guide To Papers For Envelopes, Tomoko Miho, 1971
2. Det Norske Teatret, Peter Haars, 1971
3. Earthquake, Louis Danziger, 1971
4. Maru No Osama (King Of Circles), Kiyoshi Awazu, 1971
5. Omnip In Architects, Tomoko Miho, 1971
6. Paper Airplane Book, Peter Max, 1971
7. Warsaw Autumn 1971, Hubert Hilscher, 1971
8. Milton, Kelio Rodriquez, 1971

PAGE 117
1. Van Abbemuseum, Jan van Toorn, 1971
2. Bibeb, Juriaan Schrofer, 1972
3. Roxy Music, Brian Ferry, 1972
4. The Sorrow And The Pity, Samuel Antupit, 1972
5. Randstad, TotalDesign, 1975
6. Guggenheim Museum, Chermayeff & Geismar, 1975
7. Solaris, Bertrandt Andrzej, 1972

page 118

1   2   3   4   5   6

page 119

1   2   3   4   5   6   7

page 120

1   2   3   4   5   6   7   8

page 121

1   2   3   4   5   6   7   8

page 122

1   2   3   4   5   6   7   8

PAGE 118
1. Friend Or Foe?, Tomoko Miho, 1976
2. Bicentennial USA, Massimo Vignelli, 1976
3. UCLA, Takenobu Igarashi, 1976
4. Amandla Matla - Newsletter of the African National Congress, 1977
5. Flipside Issue 001, Mr. Al, 1977
6. Who's Afraid of Frank Lloyd Wright?, Ettore Sottsass, 1977

PAGE 119
1. How To See Visual Adventures in a World God Never Made, George Nelson, 1977
2. I love NY, Milton Glaser, 1977
3. American Library Association Poster, John Massey, 1978
4. Communication, Consensus, Commitment, Tomoko Miho, 1978
5. K'Ploeng, Maarten Altena, 1978
6. Red Monarch, John Gorham, 1978
7. WET cover, April Greiman, 1979

PAGE 120
1. Leonce and Lena, Total Design, 1979
2. Visual scandals by photo montage, Tsunehisa Kimura, 1979
3. Die Gedanken sind frei, Klaus Staeck, 1979
4. HappyMeal, Seymour Chwast, 1979
5. Unknown pleasures, Peter Saville, 1979

6. Vivisection is Scientific Fraud, unknown, 1979
7. Your Name? Robot, Mikhail Romadin, 1979
8. In the Crowd, Denizens, 1980

PAGE 121
1. Buy or Die!, Gary Panter, 1980
2. Fullscale plotter billboard, Muriel Cooper, 1980
3. Geïmproviseerde Muziek, Piet Swarte, 1980
4. Get Happy!, Barney Bubbles, 1980
5. Hadi Jed, Karel Vaca, 1980
6. Maserati, Rene Gruau, 1980
7. Plankjongleur, Ewald Spieker, 1980
8. Avec l'enfant, Roman Cieslewicz, 1980

PAGE 122
1. Querelle, Andy Warhol, 1980
2. Talking Heads' Remain in Light, Tibor Kalman, 1980
3. Bring the Settlers Home, David Tartakover, 1980
4. City Art Guerilla, Ivar Vics, 1980
5. Dada in Zurich, Max Bill, 1980
6. Geisha, Ikko Tanaka, 1980
7. IBM Poster, John Anderson, 1980
8. Lulu, Franciszek Starowieyski, 1980

1   2   3   4   5   6   **7**

1   2   3   4   5   6   7   8

1   2   3   4   **5**   6   7   8

1   2   3   4   5   6   7

1   2   **3**   4   5   6

PAGE 123
1. Modellbau, Blumenstein, Plancherel & Krugel, 1980
2. Pictograms Olympic Games Moscow, Nikolai Belkow, 1980
3. Nuclear Career, Mark Vallen, 1980
4. Barney Bubbles, Barney Bubbles, 1981
5. Einsturzende Neubauten, Kollaps, 1981
6. MTV, Manhattan Design, 1981
7. Im Mittelpunkt steht immer der Mensch, Klaus Staeck, 1981

PAGE 124
1. Troilus en Cressida, Anthon Beeke, 1981
2. Brokenfingers, Bennoit Hennebert, 1982
3. De Beyerd, Jan van Toorn, 1982
4. House X, Massimo Vignelli, 1982
5. Victor of de kinderen, Jan Bons, 1982
6. Warum denn nicht frieden?, Günther Kieser, 1982
7. Tom Horn, Wlodzimierz Terechowicz, 1982
8. Unesco 1982, Rafal Olbinski, 1982

PAGE 125
1. Bally, Jacques Auriac, 1981
2. Film Im Film, Walter Pfeiffer, 1981
3. Jean-LucGodard - Filmpodium, Paul Bruhwiler, 1981
4. Rolling Stones Tattoo You, unknown, 1981
5. Exhibition Poster, Grapus, 1982

6. Jesus Raphael Soto, Almir Mavignier, 1982
7. Lugano... Citta Del Mio Cuore, Herbert Leupin, 1982
8. MKHJ - (Justus Brinckmann Geselschaft), Almir Mavignier, 1982

PAGE 126
1. IBM, Paul Rand, 1982
2. Blockhead, Barney Bubbles, 1983
3. Forget All the Rules, Bob Gill, 1983
4. Die Brennstv√§be, Rock gegen Rechts, Brennstv√§be, 1983
5. Vorsicht Kunst, Klaus Staeck, 1983
6. Grapus, 1983
7. The Modern American Poster, Chermayeff & Geismar, 1983

PAGE 128
1. Emigre #1, John Hersey, 1984
2. Legal Paper Weight, Tibor Kalman, 1984
3. Mac Icons, Susan Kare, 1984
4. Macworld, Bruce Charonnat, 1984
5. How many women had one-person exhibitions, Guerilla Girls, 1985
6. Lo-Res, Zuzana Licko, 1985

page 129

1 2 3 4 5 6 7

page 130

1 2 3 4 5 6 7 8

page 131

1 2 3 4 5 6 7 8

page 132

1 2 3 4 5 6 7

page 133

    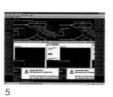 

1 2 3 4 5 6

PAGE 129
1. AIGA First National Graphic Design Conference, Carolin Warner Hightower, 1985
2. Hangul, Ahn Sang Soo, 1985
3. Next Logo, Paul Rand, 1986
4. Omo, J. Walter Thompson Company, 1986
5. Randstad, Ben Bos, 1986
6. Typograaf, Karel Treebus, 1986
7. Dangdai, He Yanming, 1986

PAGE 130
1. Measure for Measure, David Brown, 1986
2. Rape Line, Lanny Sommese, 1986
3. Reconstruction, E.K. Hudiokova, 1986
4. Sunny Murray David Murray, Niklaus Troxler, 1986
5. Typ 01, Max Kisman, 1986
6. House of Cards, Massimo Vignelli, 1987
7. Transworld Skateboarding, David Carson, 1987
8. Vrouwen eisen, Wild Plakken, 1987

PAGE 131
1. ANC, Chester Themptander, 1987
2. Before I'll drive, Bob Barrie, 1987
3. I shop therefore I am, Barbara Kruger, 1987
4. Modernism and Eclecticism, the history of american graphic design, Steven Heller, 1987

5. Tribute to Fats Waller, Niklaus Troxler, 1987
6. America's Meat Roundup, Sully & Rozier Advertising, 1988
7. De Sapeurloot, Wild Plakken, 1988
8. Tannhauser, Rick Valicenti, 1988

PAGE 132
1. High Noon, Solidarity, 1989
2. Mandela fights Apartheid, Grapus, 1989
3. Memphis, Swip Stolk, 1989
4. Obey, Shepard Fairey, 1989
5. Premiere Issue Adbusters, June Harman, 1989
6. Rats, Information Anxiety, Richard Saul Wurman, 1989
7. Romanian flag with hole, unknown, 1989

PAGE 133
1. Structures de quadrilatères, Vera Molnar, 1989
2. 1st edition Eye Magazine, Steven Coates, 1990
3. Legibility, David Carson, 1990
4. MIT medialab soft type, Muriel Cooper, 1990
5. Jodi, netart, 1990s
6. Drawingmachine, Angela Bulloch, 1991

page 134

1   2   3   4   5   6   7

page 135

1   2   3   4   5   6   7

page 136

1   2   3   4   5   6   7   8

page 137

   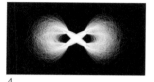

1   2   3   4   5   6

page 138

1   2   3   4   5   6   7

PAGE 134
1. Colors Magazine Issue 1, Tibor Kalman, 1991
2. Delicate Technology, Ichiro Higashiizumi, 1991
3. Emigre 19, Rudy Vanderlans, 1991
4. Laforet, Takuya Ohnuki, 1991
5. Schiphol Signage, Paul Mijksenaar, 1991
6. Slovenia, Coat of arms, Marco Pogacnik, 1991
7. The Nerd, Bob Caruthers, 1991

PAGE 135
1. Geschonden rechten, Wild Plakken, 1991
2. Legible City, Jeffrey Shaw, 1991
3. Gulf War, Prey, Jonathan Barnbrook, 1992
4. Volksbuehne, Bert Neumann, 1992
5. Existence Resistance, Ne plier pas, 1992
6. Cover of PRINT magazine, Martin Fox, 1993
7. Politie identity, Studio Dumbar, 1993

PAGE 136
1. AIGA-Los Angeles Poster, Charles S. Anderson Design Company, 1992
2. Wear a condom!, Black Dog, 1992
3. Understanding Hypermedia, Malcolm Garrett, 1992
4. "Untitled", 1992/1993, Felix González-Torres, 1992/1993
5. The 1992 Spy 100, RE, 1992
6. Star Gazers Guide, MTV Networks Creative Services, 1992

7. Rio 92, Shigeo Fukuda, 1992
8. Emigre 23 Culprits, Rudy Vanderlans & Zuzana Licko, 1992

PAGE 137
1. In the Spirit of Fluxus, Laurie Haycock & Scott Makela, 1993
2. Raygun #4, David Carson, 1993
3. Getty Images, Mark Getty, 1993
4. AI Infinity Print, John Maeda, 1994
5. Emotional Warning, True, 1994
6. Ilias, Anthon Beeke, 1994

PAGE 138
1. Diva, Paula Scher, 1994
2. Kunst Rai, Anthon Beeke, 1994
3. The History of the Blues, Carin Goldberg, 1995
4. Set the Twilight by Lou Reed, Stefan Sagmeister, 1996
5. SHV, Irma Boom, 1996
6. Blvd, Lava Grafisch Ontwerpers, 1996
7. Tibor Kalman Perverse Optimist, Michael Bierut, 1998

1

2

3

4

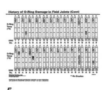
5

6

7

1

2

3

4

5

6

7

1

2

3

4

5

PAGE 131
1. Disney Go Home, James Victore Inc, 1998
2. 1948-1998, Yossi Lemel, 1998
3. Mylex 1997 Annual Report, Cahan & Associates, 1998
4. New Years Laundry Bag, @radicalmedia, 1998
5. Image from Visual Explanations, Edward R. Tufte, 1999
6. Ik ben Ben, KesselsKramer, 1999
7. Light Years, Michael Bierut, 1999

PAGE 132
1. The Bauhaus and America first contacts 1919-1936, MIT
Press Design Department, 1999
2. Emigre 51, Stephen Farrell, 1999
3. AIGA Detroit, Stefan Sagmeister, 1999
4. Julius Caesar, Hans Strybos, 1999
5. Odeur 53, Marc Atlan, 1999
6. Richard Paul Lohse Exhibition, Müller + Hess, 1999
**7. Sequoia View, TU/e Visualization Group, headed by Van
   Wijk, 1999**

PAGE 133
1. Napster Logo, Unknown, 1999
2. Tom Brochure, Diki Katona, 1999
3. The Child, H5, 1999
4. Heavens Gate America, Rick Valicenti, 1999
5. At the Start...at Long Last, Sheila Levrant de Bretteville, 1999

INDEX

GRAPHIC DESIGN 2000 - 2010

page 52

page 53

page 54

page 55

page 56

page 57

page 58 - 59

page 60

page 61

page 62

page 63

page 64

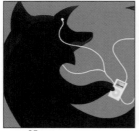
page 65

page 66

page 67

page 68

page 69

page 70 - 71

page 72

page 73

page 74

page 75

page 76

page 77

page 78

page 79

page 80 - 81

page 82

page 83

page 84

page 85

page 86 - 87

page 88

page 89

page 90

page 91

page 92

page 93

page 94 -95

page 96

page 97

page 98

page 99

page 100 - 101

page 102

page 103

page 104

page 105

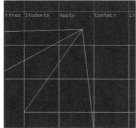

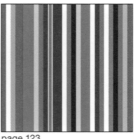

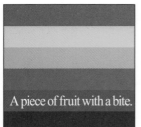

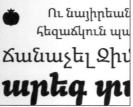

page 131

page 132

page 133

page 134

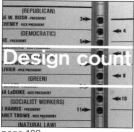

page 135

page 136

page 137

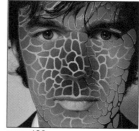

page 138

page 139

page 140

page 141

The production of this book was made possible by support of the Dioraphte Foundation,
The Province of Noord-Brabant, The City Council of Breda and The BankGiro Lottery.

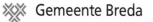

Gemeente Breda